# Connecticut in the Continental Congress

### By CHRISTOPHER COLLIER

*A Publication of*
*The American Revolution Bicentennial*
*Commission of Connecticut*

*Published by*

## PEQUOT PRESS

Chester, Connecticut

1973

ISBN: 87106-121-X
*Library of Congress Catalog Card Number:* 73–83250
*Manufactured in the United States of America*
*All Rights Reserved*
FIRST PRINTING

# Contents

# Connecticut Goes Continental

Connecticuters were always a quarrelsome people, arguing, contending, disputing, and litigating. But their quarrels were those of friends and relations, really all in the family. As bitter as they might seem at times, they lived together and worked together on the small piece of land that was Connecticut, and their fundamental instincts were collective and cooperative, not individualistic and selfish. To call their squabbling family quarrels is almost a literal truth. For colonial Connecticut was run by a collection of families so tied together by blood and marriage that any disagreement at all inevitably found family members on both sides of every question. The tribal nature of Connecticut leadership is magnificently demonstrated in the person of Ursula Wolcott who married her cousin, Matthew Griswold, and thus became the daughter, sister, wife, and mother of Connecticut governors, as well as cousin of four more of them.

Family squabbles though they may have been, Connecticuters had divided over some fairly fundamental religious and economic issues by 1765 when Parliament's fateful Stamp Act gave a new wrench to colony politics. As a result of loyalty and opposition to that Act, the breach widened and the King's supporters suffered a smashing defeat at the polls in 1766. Though efforts to regain control came close to success once or twice, the Loyalists became an increasing minority as the 1770's unfolded, and their cause collapsed with the death of their standard bearer, Thomas Fitch, in 1774. From here on, the Patriots, or Whigs as they came to be called, had it all their own way.

The problem now was to keep orderly the waxing opposition to the policies of the British home government. Mobs that had been organized and directed by second-level Whigs were useful against Stamp Act agents and persistent importers of boycotted British goods, but, if uncontrolled, these might overturn the overturners. Once having deposed the conservatives, however, the moderate Whigs were able to stem the tide of radicalism and bring revolution to Connecticut in a regulated, if unlawful, manner. When the time came for inter-colonial coordination of anti-Parliament measures, potential opponents in Connecticut (except for a pocket in western Fairfield County) had been retired from the field, though under varying degrees of duress.

The inter-colonial cooperative spirit, kindled by the Stamp Act Congress that met in New York in 1765, had been kept glowing throughout the colonies by enterprizing firebands acting more or less as individuals. But in the early 1770's they established a coordinating mechanism in town and colony Committees of Correspondence.

These committees fanned the breeze that was to inflame the nationalist spirit and result in a call for a new inter-colonial congress. The idea was first broached in Connecticut. Samuel Holden Parsons of Lyme wrote Sam Adams in March, 1773, a proposal ". . . whether it would not be advisable in the present critical situation of the colonies, to revive an institution which had formerly a very salutary effect—I mean *an annual meeting of commissioners from the colonies to consult on their general welfare.*"* Adams, however, was in no mood for congresses; what he wanted was some direct action, such as the boycott that had been so successful against the Townshend duties four years earlier.

When Parliament, as a punitive response to the Boston Tea Party, passed the extreme Coercive Acts of the spring of '74, unionist sentiment mounted rapidly, and in June the Connecticut committee wrote John Hancock that "the Colonies are all Embarked in the same general Cause, A Union in Sentiment and Measures, are of the utmost importance effectually to oppose the wicked Designs of our Common Enemies." Indeed, the month before, the Committee had urged the General Assembly to promote an inter-colonial congress. Such a congress would be a compromise between the calls from eastern towns along the Rhode Island border for a total non-importation, and declarations from conservative Fairfield County that Bostonians had destroyed the tea and they alone ought to pay for it.

But towns across the colony were becoming eager for action. Farmington town meeting termed the British cabinet "pimps and parasites" who were "instigated by the devil, and led on by their wicked and corrupt hearts," and resolved "that we scorn the chains of slavery; we despise every attempt to rivet them upon us; we are the sons of freedom . . ."; and the freemen of New Haven agreed that an inter-colonial congress "would be very agreeable to this Town . . . as soon as may be." Other towns passed similar resolutions.

On May 10, news of the Boston Port Act arrived in that offended city, and her town meeting called for inter-colonial non-importation. The Rhode Island legislature responded quickly but equivocally. She would support Boston if the other colonies would, but at the same time she called for a congress of the American colonies, and on June 15 actually elected delegates to one. Connecticut, too, disappointed the Massachusetts activists. Silas Deane, writing for the Committee of Correspondence on June 3, thought "resolves of merchants of any individual town or Province" unworkable. A "congress is absolutely necessary previous to almost every other measure, since, as the injury is

* Calls for inter-colonial congresses were, as a matter of fact, not infrequent. In 1768, at the time of the Townshend Acts, the Windham Town Meeting, "very Watchful and Jealous of our constitutional Rights and Liberties," had proposed a "General Congress."

8

general, the mode taken for redress ought to be commensurate, which is not probable to be obtained short of a general conference and union . . . the earlier . . . the better." Deane thought New York an appropriate place for such a congress, but due to the summer season approaching, a country town, he suggested, such as Norwalk or Fairfield, might be more suitable.

On the same day, the Connecticut Assembly empowered the Committee of Correspondence "to appoint a suitable number to attend such Congress or Convention of Commissioners or Committee of the several Colonies in British America . . . to consult and advise on proper measures for advancing the best good of the Colonies. . . ." Thus Connecticut anticipated the Rhode Island election by almost two weeks, and became the first colony to authorize appointments, though Rhode Island actually *elected* hers first.

Eight of the nine-man Committee met in New London on July 13, 1774, and appointed three of its own members, Silas Deane, Eliphalet Dyer, and Erastus Wolcott, along with William S. Johnson and Richard Law, to be delegates to the Congress. But the two non-members refused to serve, as did Wolcott who must have been absent at his election. Wolcott and Law, both temperamentally cautious, pleaded illness, and Johnson, who wrote to a friend in England that he "did not think it advisable either on my own acct., or that of the Colony to make one of that Assembly," lied to the Committee that "previous engagements" forbade acceptance of the appointment. Johnson knew that it was ". . . very unpopular of present to doubt in any measure either the legality or expediency of the measure," and his retirement from politics for the duration of the war was mutually agreeable to him and the Connecticut freemen.

But the resignations created problems, for factions had developed within the Committee of Correspondence. On one side were the three thirty-seven year old activists—Deane, Joseph Trumbull, and his Harvard classmate, Samuel Parsons. On the other were the older men: Samuel Bishop of New Haven, William Williams of Lebanon, forty-four and forty-three, and old Ebenezer Siliman of Fairfield, who was sixty-seven.

Since it took three delegates to represent the colony, it was thought necessary to appoint at least one more, but preferably two. On August 1, the Committee of Correspondence met again, and Silas Deane spilled the beans of factionalism to William S. Johnson.

> The meeting of the Committee yesterday was very curious indeed, there were Eight of Us and schemers too you may well conclude, when you are informed that in order to lead off, from a Gentleman to the Eastward, it was insisted that a man at the Westward should be Nominated, the reasons urged were in sum this, That it would tend to quiet the Minds of the People by an equal location—Four of the Committee for Four

against such a Measure....A vote was called and Mr. Sherman had Four for Four against, after repeated tryals they conferred....Finally as a compromise was made that We could nominate two, One of which should attend, on this Mr. Sherman and Capt. Trumbull were Nominated —Now it is very much left with Mr. Sherman, as he stands first in Nomination to determine the Matter and here I must ask you to say one word...wish if consistent with your delicacy that you would hint your Sentiments to this good Gentleman, on the Subject—I have most sincerely a high Opinion of that good Gentleman in the Capacity of a Judge, and a Magistrate...and I am of the opinion that Such a weakening of the Court will give great general umbrage, which I plainly see will turn in part on Us the Committee, and possibly in part on him, and I am sure he is not solicitous for the post.

Though perhaps "not solicitous for the post," Sherman had his share of both patriotism and vanity and did indeed choose to go. "I wish," wrote worried William S. Johnson, "they may be cool and wise." Cool and wise certainly was Roger Sherman. Aloof, reserved, and even severe are the words most often used to describe this self-educated surveyor, lawyer, and mathematician. Crafty, slippery, sly, and clever are others frequently found next to his name, too. Taciturn among his family and friends, but talkative on the public stage, Thomas Jefferson called him "a man who never said a foolish thing in his life." Sherman indeed was the archetypal Puritan Yankee. Though he appeared moderate in his manner and demeanor, his views were radical; as early as 1766 Sherman was wondering how long the colonial connection would continue. His concepts of Connecticut's role in the world fit so completely those of Patriot leaders from other colonies that he was at perfect peace with the independence men of '75 and '76. The Adams' and Lees' considered him one of the family.

Sherman was the most influential of all Connecticut statesmen during the entire Congressional period, 1774–1789, and beyond. He served longer and more continuously than any other, and sat on more committees and wrote more reports than almost any man from all the colonies. Alone he claims the title as "The Great Signer." He signed the Association establishing the inter-colonial boycott of British goods, the Declaration of Rights of 1774, the Declaration of Independence, the Articles of Confederation, the Peace of Paris of 1783, and the Constitution of 1787. No other man put his name to even four of these six documents. His success in bringing things around his way was due to his incisive intellect and his extraordinary ability to develop compromise positions in backstage conversation. He spoke often, but simply, in public and, despite his rough manner, must have been persuasive. "Sherman's air is the reverse of grace," wrote John Adams in 1775,

there cannot be a more striking contrast to beautiful action, than the motions of his hands; generally he stands upright, with his hands before

*10*

him, the fingers of his left hand clenched into a fist, and the wrist of it grasped with his right. But he has a clear head and sound judgment; but when he moves a hand in any thing like action, Hogarth's genious could not have invented a motion more opposite to grace;—it is stiffness and awkwardness itself, rigid as starched linen or buckram; awkward as a junior or sophomore.

Probably Sherman was not very scintillating company, but to Silas Deane he was a crashing bore or worse. Of course, Deane had no use for the rough old fellow to begin with, and had connived to keep him out of the delegation. But Deane was Yale-educated and trying hard to rise above the blacksmith's situation that was his father's. A pair of very profitable marriages had provided a solid base from which to launch a successful mercantile career. However, he had been one of the most active of those Connecticuters who were trying to keep up the old boycott of British goods in the early seventies. In that capacity he was a frequent correspondent of New York and New England merchants, and as secretary to the Council of Safety in 1773 and 1774, he continued these connections.

Once in Philadelphia, Deane became a leading figure in Congress and served on numerous military committees. He had excellent executive ability developed through his mercantile experience, and was a tremendously energetic and successful organizer. "I rise at six," he wrote his wife, "write until seven, dress and breakfast by eight, go to the Committee of Claims until ten; then in Congress till half-past three or perhaps four; dine by five, and then go either to the Committee of Secrecy, or of Trade until nine; then sup and go to bed by eleven. This leaves little room for diversion or anything else. . . ."

Deane's tremendously energetic and aggressive entrepreneurship found expression in Connecticut's strange effort to annex the northern tier of Pennsylvania which lay along the Susquehannah River. He was inspired by the launching of this great land scheme, in which he appears to have been involved as early as 1752 at the age of fifteen, and in 1774 he was writing flamboyant propaganda tracts for the Susquehannah Company. By this time, Governor Trumbull, father of Deane's close friend Joseph, was thoroughly involved in Susquehannah affairs. It is noteworthy that Eliphalet Dyer was the principal leader of the Company in Connecticut, so that, had Deane been successful in replacing Sherman with Joseph Trumbull, the delegation could have been a solid Susquehannah phalanx. There is no question that Connecticut's claim to a large piece of Pennsylvania lands was a major factor in Deane's eagerness to establish a colonial congress free of British restrictions.

Mr. Susquehannah himself was the first Connecticut delegate named by the Committee of Correspondence in the exciting hot summer of '74. Eliphalet Dyer came from Windham, probably the colony's most radical town, where he had been practicing law since shortly after his graduation from Yale in 1740. Six months younger than Roger Sherman, Dyer was everything that the ex-cobbler was not. Sophisticated not only by classical education, but also through travel, Dyer, wrote James Madison, was "a man of gentlemanly manners, who had seen the world." But to Connecticut's conservatives he was something else. As leader of the Susquehannah movement he bent all his efforts to assure its success, and thus became the most controversial Patriot in the Colony. Dyer did indeed make himself ridiculous sometimes by his hot pursuit of legality for the Company's claims. One of his colleagues in the Connecticut lower house during a particularly flamboyant harangue, penned:

> Cannan of old, as we are told
> When it did rain down manna
> Wa'nt half so good, for heavenly food
> As Dyer makes Susquehannah

"It is well known," Dyer admitted to a close friend, that "I am warm, impetuous and perservering."

Certainly there is no question about his perseverance. A hostile Pennsylvanian claimed that Dyer spoke "twenty times a day, and scarcely ever finishes one sentence completely." Honest John Adams, however, provided a more balanced picture: "Dyer," he wrote, "is long-winded and round-about, obscure and cloudy, very talkative and very tedious, yet an honest, worthy man, means and judges well."

Dyer accumulated a good fortune through his legal practice and sundry business endeavors, kept slaves, and tried to live as much like the British aristocracy as was possible in provincial Windham. He knew a little bit about how that was done, for he spent most of 1764 in London courting the favor of the Crown on behalf of his "darling Susquehannah." There, he wrote, "I make a point of it allmost every week to make an appearance att Court att St. James . . . present King, Queen, the Royal family, Nobility, Gentry etc. . . . at Church once a Week, at play near as often."

He was unsuccessful in England, became disgusted with the tedious deviousness of Whitehall, and, since his visit coincided with the rising spirit of repressive imperialism there, gained first-hand some insight into a frightening future for the American colonies. A pompous provincial, perhaps, but not stupid, Dyer wrote home that the ministry "seems determined to fix upon us a large Number of regular Troops under pretence for our Defence; but rather designed as a rod and Check over us, and are determined to raise a fund in America for their Support. . . ." When it came time for the General Assembly to elect delegates to the Stamp Act Congress in 1765, Dyer was the most

12

obvious choice, and later he would find eight of his Stamp Act colleagues at Congress in 1774.

Besides their close association in the Susquehannah affair, Dyer and Deane were temperamentally not too dissimilar, and their views of society, despite a sixteen year age difference, were relatively akin. John Adams wrote of Deane that "he was a person of a plausible readiness and Volubility with his tongue and Pen, much adicted to Ostentation and Expense in Dress and Living but without any deliberate forcast or reflection or solidity of judgement, or real Information." Dyer, at the eve of the trio's second journey to Philadelphia the next year, would beg a ride in Deane's "Leathern Conveniency" where "we can Chatt, we can sing, we can dispute everything. Scold and make friends again every half hour." One wonders how dour Roger Sherman who "never said a foolish thing in his life" would enjoy their company.

In any event, ruffle-cuffed Dyer and Deane took the short-haired Roger with them when they left Connecticut for Philadelphia on a hot August 24, 1774. Along the way the delegates were entertained by the gentlemen of the towns, and in the major cities crowds were waiting to escort them to their lodgings and to provide them with great ceremonial banquets. A few days of this and Sherman was beginning to wear a bit on finicky Silas Deane, who confided to his wife: "Mr. Sherman is clever in private, but I can only say he is as badly calculated to appear in such a Company as a Chestnut-burr is for an eyestone. He occasioned some shrewd countenances among the company, and not a few oaths, by the odd questions he asked, and the very odd and countrified cadence with which he speaks; but he was, and did, as well as I expected." The next day, however, the store of Deane's patience was drawn on again by his Puritan colleague. "Mr. Sherman (would to Heaven he were well at New Haven,) is against our sending our carriages over the ferry this evening, because it is Sunday; so we shall have a scorching sun to drive forty miles in tomorrow." A couple of weeks later Deane was still rehashing the miseries of the trip to his wife. "As I suspected our delay or rather superstitious neglect of getting over our Carriage the preceding evening, brought us under the mercy of the ferryman, who kept us until after ten that excessive hot day, and then part of us, not myself for one assisted in rowing over." Stopping to visit a friend in Trenton, Deane continued, "I never underwent more to keep up my part of the conversation," so sick was he with dysentery. "But so it was, I could not retire until past eleven, when, as fond as I am of sleep, the night and bed were worse to me than to have proceeded on my journey. I turn'd and turn'd, and groan'd while Judge Sherman who lodged in the same chamber snored in concert." The miseries were shortly over, however, for on September 1 the delegates arrived in Philadelphia, and it was time to buckle down to work.

# The First Continental Congress

THE Connecticut delegation arrived at Philadelphia "in high spirits," Deane told his wife, adding, "if it is possible to be really so when the eyes of millions are upon us. . . ." Within four days, a majority of colony delegations had assembled, and they gathered on Monday, September 5, 1774, at the City Tavern. Lines between conservatives and radicals were quickly defined by the Pennsylvania delegation which split over the presumably routine question of where to convene. Carpenters' Hall was chosen over the State House, which had been offered by the Pennsylvania Speaker, Joseph Galloway. This was a victory for the radicals. As Silas Deane explained Galloway's offer, the State House "is evidently the best place, but as *he* offers, the other party oppose." Without a dissenting vote, Peyton Randolph of Virginia was chosen chairman, or president as he was styled, but a contest arose over the secretaryship. The conservatives wished to appoint from within Congress, and put up the name of Silas Deane, while the radicals supported a non-member, Charles Thompson, the "Sam Adams of Philadelphia." Perhaps the conservatives thought they could carry the vote by nominating the fiery Deane; perhaps there were other considerations in which Deane figured less passively. He wrote his wife that "it was a matter of dispute whether we should choose a Secretary out[side] of the Members, and I doubted in my own mind the propriety, but did not oppose it, as by opposing I probably should have had the task myself, which is too burdensome to one who wants all spare hours for relaxation." So he lost, and the radicals had a second victory.

One more question had to be settled before any business could be done. This was the sticky problem of the relative weight of each colony's vote. Should more populous colonies get proportional votes; or should there be equality among them? Virginia, Pennsylvania, and Massachusetts were determined on proportions; but the others were not. Connecticut was a middle-sized colony, ranking, it was thought at the time, fifth, just a bit larger than sixth-place New York. Fifth out of thirteen could have put the Connecticut delegates in league with the large states, but no contingent was to be more steadfast throughout the whole period in its insistence on a one-state-one-vote system. In 1774 they had their way.

At bottom, the division in the Congress of 1774 lay between those desiring to deal with Great Britain through petition alone, and those wishing to effect a program of action to give backbone to their petitions. Specifically, the parties opposed each other on: 1) the theoretical grounds upon which to base their opposition to Parliamentary measures; 2) whether to establish inter-colonial trade restrictions against England; 3) how to act upon the inflammatory Suffolk Resolves sent down from Boston. The Connecticut delegation, despite Deane's flirtation with the conservatives, was emphatic and unambiguous on each of these.

The first question was fundamental. Did American Englishmen derive their rights from that collection of statute, proclamation, tradition, and judicial decision known as the British Constitution, along with the colonial charters; or was there a higher law of nature that defined and limited the powers of government? Joseph Galloway stated the conservative view of the situation. His faction, he said, "intended candidly and clearly to define American rights, and explicitly and dutifully to petition for the remedy . . . a more solid and constitutional union between the two countries." The other group, he declared not too inaccurately, consisted of "persons whose design, from the beginning of their opposition to the Stamp Act, was to throw off all subordination and connexion with Great Britain; who meant by every fiction, falsehood and fraud, to delude the people from their due allegiance to throw the subsisting governments into anarchy, to incite the ignorant and vulgar to arms, and with those arms to establish American independence." Galloway was shortly to grow disillusioned with the state of American politics and move to England where he was to become the chief spokesman of the American Loyalists. He could not have been happy with the Connecticut position.

Three months earlier, back in Connecticut the General Assembly had declared allegiance to the King, but held as "an indispensible duty" to him and "to our country, ourselves, and our posterity, by all lawful ways and means in our power, to maintain, defend and preserve these our rights and liberties, and to transmit them entire and inviolate to the latest generation; . . . it is our fixed, determined and unalterable resolution faithfully to discharge this our duty." And to leave no doubt in the minds of the Parliamentary adversaries, the Assembly stated its view that these rights, those of all freeborn Englishmen, were theirs "by the laws of nature, by the royal grant and charter . . ., and by long and uninterrupted possession." The Assembly explicitly included freedom from taxation except by themselves, the right to local self-government, trials by local juries, and freedom from arbitrary closure of ports and harbors as rights recognized and confirmed by the royal charter of 1662. The Connecticut Congressional delegates, of course, had had a hand in the writing of the resolution, and they faced no problems of conscience in supporting the principles expressed.

Eliphalet Dyer, after witnessing first-hand the development of British colonial policy while in London in 1764, had provided a sharp insight and an early warning. The colonies, he wrote Governor Fitch at that time, "may for the future, bid Farewell to Freedom and Liberty, burn their Charters, and make the best of thraldom and slavery. For if we can have our Interest and Estate taken away, and disposed of without our consent, or having any voice therein. . . . why may they not as well endeavor to raise Millions upon us to dafray the Expenses of the last, or any Future War?" Roger Sherman had written in 1772: "It is a fundamental principle in the British Constitution and I think it must be in every free State, that no laws bind the people but such as they consent to be governed by, therefore so far as the people of the Colonies are bound by laws made without their consent, they must be in a state of slavery or absolute subjection to the will of others. . . ." Parliamentary policy, if countenanced in regard to Boston, meant slavery for the colonists everywhere: Connecticuters were convinced of that. Their "Darling Charter" had given them virtual autonomy for more than a century, and they represented a tradition of self-government stronger than any of their sister colonies. "The Colonies," Sherman declared in floor debate, "are not bound to the King or Crown by the act of settlement, but by their consent to it. There is no other legislative over the Colonies but their respective assemblies." British policy threatened real local self-government, and traditional virtues of a frugal, simple life-style. Not only would the Ministry subvert republican political institutions, but through its corrupt emissaries to the colonies it would spread luxury and dissipation among the plain-living American yeomen.

The Declaration of Rights that Congress drafted fell short of the Connecticut position. It included the concession that "we cheerfully consent to the operation of such acts of the British parliament as are bona fide restrained to the regulation of our external commerce, for the purpose of securing the commercial advantages of the whole empire to the mother country, and the commercial benefits of its respective members excluding every idea of taxation, internal or external, for raising a revenue on the subjects in America without their consent." Roger Sherman had been of the opinion for at least a couple of years that "tho' some general Regulation of Trade &c. may be necessary for the General Interest of the nation. . . ." there was, nevertheless, "no constitutional way to establish such regulations so as to be legally binding upon the people of the several distinct Dominions . . . but by the consent of the Legislature of each Government." But the Connecticut view represented the vanguard, and they could not have everything their own way. Along with the other New England delegations, Sherman, Dyer, and Deane were content to wait a bit and let the rest of the colonies catch up. The "Declaration and Resolves," however, was no weak document. It asserted a strong claim to all the traditional rights of Englishmen, including the right to keep life, liberty, and property; to assemble and petition; to jury trials; to local self-government; and freedom from standing armies and arbitrary proclamations.

Events were rushing the Congress toward decision faster than many members cared to go, but too slowly for others. Events can be managed, however, and Sam Adams, the chief manager, knew how to keep the pressure on. From Adams' home county of Suffolk came a set of resolves penned by his lieutenant, Dr. Joseph Warren. The county convention expressed them by Paul Revere down to Philadelphia where they were dropped as a bombshell on Carpenters' Hall. The preamble alone disgusted the conservatives who saw its bombast as a painful vexation. "If we arrest the hand which would ransack our pockets," wrote Warren, doomed to die at Bunker Hill,

> if we disarm the parracide which points the dagger to our bosoms, . . . if we successfully resist that unparalleled usurpation of unconstitutional power, whereby our capital is robbed of the means of life; whereby the streets of Boston are thronged with military executioners; whereby our coasts are lined and harbours crowded with ships of war; whereby the charter of the colony, that sacred barrier against the encroachments of tyranny, is mutilated and, in effect, annihilated; whereby a murderous law is framed to shelter villains from the hands of justice; whereby the unalienable and inestimable inheritance, which we derived from nature, the constitution of Britain, and the privileges warranted to us in the charter of the province is totally wrecked, annulled, and vacated, posterity will acknowledge that virtue which preserved them free and happy; . . . .

As treasonous as the rhetoric was, the real danger, the conservatives saw, came in the program of action proposed. This was to ignore the intolerable Parliamentary acts against Boston; to reorganize the militia, purging it of officers holding commissions under the British government; to stop all commerce with Great Britain immediately; and to refrain from consuming British goods. The whole thing, said Galloway, was "a complete declaration of war against Great Britain." So it may have seemed to Galloway and his conservative friends. But not to the Connecticut delegation. Sherman, for one, had years before stated his view that Parliament's claim to authority to legislate for the colonies in *all* cases whatsoever ought to be reversed: it had such authority in *no* case whatsoever, he would have it. It was easy for him and his colleagues, Dyer and Deane, to support the Suffolk Resolves and vote with the Congressional majority for approval of "the wisdom and fortitude" of the Massachusetts leaders.

Perhaps mere declarations were considered of less importance at this juncture than concrete action. The time had come to call the hand of the timorous and indecisive. How would the Congress respond to a real program, one that would not only be considered illegal by the

home government, but one that would flatten the pocketbooks of some
of the delegates and many of their friends as well? An economic strike
against England had been a radical aim from the start. Indeed, conservatives had welcomed a Congress as a more palatable protest than
a boycott. But conservative success was only apparent, for the radicals
controlled the Congress and put their program across. There was considerable debate, however, on the nature of the boycott. Should there
be a general nonintercourse with England, or merely nonimportation
and nonconsumption? Connecticut people would not be nearly so
agitated about this as would the commercial colonies. She imported
very little from England or, indeed, from any transatlantic ports. Her
trade was West Indian and coastal, with European goods transshipped
through New York, Newport, and Boston.

A Connecticut correspondent assumed that Deane would be for
both nonimportation and nonexportation, but had heard that Sherman
might be opposed to both. The pragmatic Sherman knew that ultimately materiel of various sorts would have to be purchased from
across the Atlantic, and that produce must leave America in exchange.
Perhaps a limited program would be the most practical, especially
since southerners were so dependent upon English purchases of to-
bacco, rice, and other commodities. But the radicals had their way,
and a total boycott of British goods was established, along with a nonexportation to England and her possessions of all commodities except
rice, South Carolina's economic mainstay.

To enforce this commercial program, Congress established the
Continental Association, and set dates for initiating various parts of the
boycott: December 1 for nonimportation; March 1, 1775, for nonconsumption; and September 10 for nonexportation. The Association,
in turn, called for the creation of committees in every "county, city,
and town" in America to see to its implementation. Connecticut, Silas
Deane· promised Sam Adams, would "pay the most sacred regard to
the resolutions of the Congress."

Deane spoke for most of his constituents, but not for all. Fairfield
County, with its many members of the Church of England and its
proximity to Tory-ridden New York City and Westchester County, had
numerous pockets of dissent to the new rebel consensus. Ridgefield,
for example, split geographically with the Loyalist center against the
Patriots in Ridgebury. The official town meeting declared allegiance to
the King and vowed to "support his throne and dignity against every
combination in the universe"; but the Ridgebury Liberty Men voted
overwhelming approval of the Association. Some Newtown citizens
followed Ridgefield in a set of resolutions nearly word for word the
same, but they, too, met opposition from a collection of their towns-
fellows who expressed themselves "deeply apprehensive that [the
Coercive Acts] are of a very unconstitutional and oppressive nature

in their tendency, directly subversive of [our] precious rights and privileges . . .," and they expressed support of the Congress.

In Redding there were more Tories than Patriots. The Loyalists preempted the initiative and formed themselves into their own Association to combat what they saw as calculated promotion of confusion and disorder. They supposed, they said, that "the Continental Congress was constituted for the purpose of restoring harmony between Great Britain and her colonies and removing the displeasure of his Majesty toward his American subjects, whereas on the contrary some of their resolutions appear to us immediately calculated to widen the present unhappy breach, counteract the first principles of civil society, and in a great degree abridge the privileges of their constituents." The Loyalist Association would, their declaration insisted, "defend, maintain and preserve at the risk of our lives and properties the prerogatives of the Crown, and the privileges of the subject from all attacks by any rebellious body of men, any Committees of Inspection, Correspondence, &c."

These places, however, were out of step with the rest of Connecticut. The Assembly, at a special session in March, listened to Governor Trumbull inveigh against "depraved Malignant, aviricious and haughty" minded Tories, and then proceeded to set up committees to investigate the western towns. It also endorsed the action of Congress in respect to the Association and ordered each town to establish committees of inspection. More typical than the Ridgefield fracas was the expeditious action of Fairfield where the Committee of Inspection prepared a statement "in order to subscribe an Association, to show that they are the friends to the liberties and privileges of their Country, and that the enemies of it may be known." They collected the signatures of 855 males over sixteen, and found only seventy who would not subscribe—and those names they published to the world. Ridgefield, Redding, and Newtown were boycotted by most of the rest of the towns, and by the Assembly as well.

Connecticut faced two major problems in enforcing the terms of the Association. One was the proximity of Long Island and Tory-dominated New York. Countless Connecticut farmers were tempted by the high prices paid for beef, sheep, and produce in those places, and made efforts to get their crops and livestock there. This trade continued throughout the war, though great efforts were made to stop it. A whaleboat navy was established specifically for the purpose, but in southwestern Fairfield County there were so many Tories, and it was so easy to trade with the high-paying enemy, that collusion often occurred and Connecticut produce found its way unimpeded to the British at New York City. But as far as transatlantic shipping and transshipment of British goods into Connecticut was concerned, the Yankee state probably effected a stoppage as well as any other.

Nonconsumption, however, was a different matter. One Killingworth skeptic pointed out that most of the towns west of the Connecticut River had organized no committees to carry out any kind of anti-Parliamentary program. Though compliance in the eastern counties appears to have been voluntary and quite universal, in Fairfield and adjoining counties constant vigilance and inspection was necessary to keep miscreants clean. Names of violators of the agreements were published in newspapers; recalcitrants were tarred and feathered and in other ways intimidated. "What? Do you drink tea?" wrote a committee member in the *New Haven Gazette*, "Take care what you do, . . . for you are to know the committee commands the mob and can in an instance let them loose upon any man, who opposes their decree, and complete his destruction." Ultimately, with the development of war-inspired patriotism and the flight of hundreds of the most willful Loyalists, nonconsumption was made fairly effective throughout the state. Compliance with Congressional resolutions was not always taken so seriously, but in the case of the Continental Association a strenuous effort was made.

The First Continental Congress sat from September 5 to October 26. Its tone had been firm but generally moderate, and the action program limited to economic sanctions. But before it adjourned, a date for another meeting was set for May 10, 1775. And by that time the patriot temper had changed, for blood had been spilled on Lexington Green.

## Generals and Politicians

THE Second Continental Congress was, in its early days, virtually a repetition of the First in its personnel. Fifty-five members had served the previous fall, and only four delegates to the First were not returned to the Second. Benjamin Franklin, James Wilson, John Hancock and Thomas Jefferson were among the new members. This time, Georgia, unrepresented in the First Congress, sent one delegate, Lyman Hall, originally of Wallingford, Connecticut. From Connecticut itself would come the doughty trio, Sherman, Dyer, and Deane.

The Connecticut delegates were to be well primed for the constitutional issues that had arisen. The General Assembly statement of October, 1774, was given added emphasis by Governor Trumbull, who declared that "the good people" of Connecticut were "unfeignedly loyal, and firmly attached to His Majesty's person, family and Government," and expressed hope for "a speedy and happy settlement upon constitutional grounds." But, he insisted, "it will be admitted that it is our duty, and that we should be even highly culpable, if we should not claim and maintain the constitutional rights and liberties derived to us as men and *Englishmen;* as descendants of *Britons,* and members of an Empire whose fudamental principle is the liberty and security of the subject." The Governor also suggested that good relations between England and America could be resumed only when the troops had left Boston, and Massachusetts had been returned to her former self-governing status.

Constitutional principles became of less immediate concern, however, when the King declared that "the New England governments are now in a state of rebellion; blows must decide whether they are to be subject to this country or independent." Troops were ordered out to capture the Boston ring leaders, Hancock and Adams, and to destroy militia supplies at Concord. The constitutional argument, finally, was to be decided by force of arms.

Word of Lexington and Concord reached eastern Connecticut on April 20, 1775, and swept across the colony over the next two days. The news steeled the Connecticut delegates and added not only weight to their impending deliberations, but also excitement and glamor to their persons. The "leathern conveniency" of Deane's carried them from Wethersfield to New Haven and on to Stamford where they picked up a horse guard to new York City. They had been joined by the Massachusetts delegates, who were now taking on something of an heroic character, and the whole group went from town to town and entertainment to entertainment, greeted everywhere by joyous and noisy tumults. They reached Philadelphia on May 10, and "were met," wrote Deane to his wife, "at about six miles on this side of the City by about two hundred of the principal gentlemen on horseback with their swords drawn. . . . At about two miles distance we were met by a Company on foot, and then by a Company of Riflemen in their uniforms which is very curious. Thus rolling and gathering like a snowball, we approached the City, which was full of people and the crowd as great as at New York, the bells all ringing and the air rent with shouts and huzzas." But serious business awaited the Connecticut trio at Philadelphia. "The scenes before us are so vast," wrote Deane to his wife, ". . . I tremble when I think of their vast importance. May the God of Wisdom preside."

Connecticut provided the Congress with its happiest piece of work during the initial days of the second session. The never-idle Silas Deane, along with the able and ambitious Samuel Holden Parsons and other members of the Connecticut Council of War, as the old Committee of Correspondence now styled itself, had devised a military scheme in concert with Ethan Allen, formerly of Litchfield, Connecticut. Allen at this time lived in the New Hampshire Grants where he was a major speculator in lands claimed simultaneously by New York and New Hampshire. The strategic "key to the gateway to the continent" from Canada south was an old French fort situated on a promontory one hundred feet above the spilling waters of Lake George at a point where passage to Lake Champlain is but a quarter of a mile wide. The fort, at what the Iroquois called the "place between the big waters," or Ticonderoga, was in bad repair and garrisoned by about fifty men, many of them ill. Benedict Arnold was under the impression that there were about 400 men at the Fort, but there was a prize there, he told Parsons as they met on their way to Cambridge at the time of the Lexington Alarm: about eighty cannons, just what was needed to blow Gage out of Boston. Deane and Parsons persuaded the Connecticut Council of War to provide £300, mostly from private donation, and assembled a small party to contact Ethan Allen who was the commander of a group of vigilantes organized to terrorize New York settlers and officials who attempted to oust them from the lands. Allen delighted in the assignment and led his Green Mountain Boys to Ticonderoga and the smaller post just a bit to the north at Skenesboro, both of which fell in a matter of minutes.

The capture of Ticonderoga and its handy cannons took place on May 10, 1775, the very day that Congress was reconvening in Philadelphia. The news arrived a week later and was the first order of business the next morning. The Congress, as striking evidence of the still-prevailing ambivalence about American objectives, resolved that the fort should be abandoned! The stores and guns were to be removed, of course, but a complete inventory was to be taken "in order that they may be safely returned when the restoration of the former harmony between Great Britain and these colonies so ardently wished for by the latter shall render it prudent."

To stop at the Lake posts was one thing; to abandon them quite another. The New England delegates in Congress, particularly the Connecticut delegation with "Ticonderoga" Deane sparking it, would not accept the weaseling response of the majority. The Connecticut Council of Safety, always in close touch with its Congressmen, determined to go ahead on its own if necessary, and word of this threat persuaded Congress to change its mind. The victory at Ticonderoga was an important one. Many of the captured guns were too dilapidated to salvage, but seventy-eight of them, ranging from four to twenty-eight pounders, were in good shape. Six mortars, three howitzers, thousands of cannon balls, nine tons of musket bullets, thirty thousand flints, and a vast array of other military apparatus quickly provided the essential elements of Washington's siege of Boston. The daring initiative and decisive action of Connecticut's Council of Safety, and the military aggressiveness of several of her officers, put her in the forefront of the colonial cause. Only the delegates from beleaguered Massachusetts enjoyed greater reputation in Congressional circles than Silas Deane and his Connecticut colleagues; ". . . not only the name of a *Yankee*, but of a Connecticut man in particular, is become very respectable this way . . .," he wrote to the folks back home.

The fighting around Boston and the Lakes had been carried on under the aegis of the extralegal Committees of Safety of Massachusetts and Connecticut. Now it was time to get organized. Congress was a no more legal body than either of these little units, but revolutions are carried on under the banner of morality, not legality, and a concerted stance would strengthen the moral conviction of nervous New Englanders. Besides, an army organized on an inter-colonial basis would be much stronger and much more efficient. For provincial Connecticuters, however, there were problems as well as promises in the prospect of a unified army. Politics and personalities would have to take precedence over merit, or the whole thing might shatter in the process of creation.

About fifteen thousand men, three thousand of them from Connecticut, hovered on the hills that lay crescent-like around Boston. They were half-trained men and untrained boys, accustomed to the election of company officers and unused to the unreasoning military discipline bred into the professional soldier. The Massachusetts troops were under command of Artemas Ward, a French and Indian War veteran. New Hampshire troops had formally placed themselves under his command, and the Connecticut commanders were willing and cooperative. But despite cooperation at the top, the junior officers disputed among themselves and with their superiors, and the men were wont to control the officers who rose to rank by popular election. They faced about sixty-five hundred British regulars holed up in town with large reinforcements on the way.

Efficiency called for a unified command, and politics called for Congressional supervision, if the New Englanders were to make their Boston battle a continental war. The Massachusetts Provincial Congress wrote to Philadelphia on May 16 that "the sword should, in all free States, be subservient to the civil powers. . . . we tremble at having an Army (although consisting of our own countrymen) established here, without a civil power to provide for and control them. . . . We would beg leave to suggest to your consideration," the beleaguered but crafty Massachusetts leaders continued, "the propriety of your taking the regulation and general direction of it, that the operations of it may more effectually answer the purpose designed." This was a touchy business for Congressmen from south of Byram River. Were they to involve their colonies in the bloody business now engaging the too-republican New Englanders? But Congress had already authorized Connecticut to garrison the Lake forts, and New York to erect barriers on the Hudson River. And hadn't it just requested the New Englanders to provide Ward's Boston troops with powder, ball, and provisions?

The Massachusetts invitation arrived at Philadelphia on June 2, 1775, and was put off for the day. Silas Deane was cautiously optimistic. Though Congress, he thought, was "a very unwieldy Body . . . unanimity . . . hitherto prevails to a most surprising degree." John Adams was provoked that Congress, as it continued another week of debate on the Massachusetts question, insisted that it "keep open the Door of Reconciliation to hold the sword in one Hand and the olive Branch in the other." But, he sighed, "this Continent is a vast, unwieldy Machine. We cannot force Events." But by June 10 the handwriting was at least on the wall, if not in official dispatches, for Congress did vote to raise £6000 to purchase powder. Four days later the other shoe was finally dropped, and the New Englanders knew they would not fight alone. Congress agreed to raise an army drawn from all those colonies able to provide men immediately.

Twenty thousand troops to march to Boston from Pennsylvania, Virginia, and Maryland was a magnificent offering, and John Adams knew how to cement the relationship. How would his fellow New Englanders feel about putting the whole thing, Artemas Ward and all the Connecticut, New Hampshire, and Rhode Island militia, under a general from Virginia? Roger Sherman was aghast. A New England army must have a New England commander. He received some support from Thomas Cushing of Massachusetts and Edmund Pendleton of Virginia. But Adams' stroke was too brilliant to be deflected by personal and provincial jealousies, and the nomination of George Washington was made unanimous on June 15.* Deane, a burgeoning nationalist, and Dyer, with his cosmopolitan veneer, immediately saw the merit in the idea if not the man. "I don't believe," wrote Dyer about the new commander-in-chief, "as to his Military & for real service he

---

* Not yet apprised of this action, the Connecticut Council of Safety on the 19th voted that "the Governor be advised to give orders to our officers and soldiers to be subordinate and yield obedience to the general and commanding officer of the troops of the Massachusetts Bay, while they act in that Province. . . ." At the same time, General David Wooster's troops in New York were placed "under the direction of the Continental Congress and of the Congress of said Province of New York. . . ." He objected to the latter body: "I have no faith in their honesty in the cause," he wrote Trumbull. "I must, therefore, think it not only a disgrace to me, but a dishonor to my employers, that I am subjected to them. You know not, Sir, half their tricks." On October 15, the General Assembly placed the troops on campaign in Canada and those with Schuyler in New York under "regulations and discipline of the Congress of the twelve united Colonies. . . ." In December, the old militia drill, the Norfolk Militia Exercise, was given up for the Manual Exercise which was in use by the Continental Army.

knows more than some of ours . . .," but he is "Clever, and if anything too modest. He seems discreet and Virtuous, no harum starum ranting swearing fellow but sober, steady and Calm." These were characteristics, he knew, that would make Washington "very Agreeable to the Genius and Climate of New England." Silas Deane, after spending two days in close consultation with Washington, believed that "the more I am acquainted with [him], the more I esteem him. . . ." Deane, who always knew a good thing when he saw it, sat right down and wrote his close collaborator, Joseph Trumbull, then at camp near Cambridge, "immediately on his Appointment I took the Liberty . . . of recommending You to him, as his Secretary, for which an hansome Appointment is made by Congress." But Washington chose instead Joseph Reed, president of Pennsylvania's Provincial Congress. There would be more plums to be picked, and Joseph Trumbull would get his soon enough.

Upon receipt of the news of Lexington and Concord, which reached his house on the Lebanon Green shortly after noon on April 20, 1775, Governor Jonathan Trumbull had convened a special session of the General Assembly in order to organize the militia for its task of supporting the Massachusetts forces around Boston. The Assembly then provided for the enlisting and equipping of one-fourth of the militia, about six thousand men, to be organized into six regiments to serve for seven months—until the regular October session. Two more regiments were added in July.

Long involvement in Britain's colonial wars had provided the American colonies with numerous well-experienced officers, and Connecticut had her share of some of the most distinguished. First among these was David Wooster of New Haven. He had served as an officer aboard a coast guard sloop during England's war with Spain in the 1740's, and later was commissioned captain of a company of militia raised for the seige of Louisburg. He was placed in charge of prisoners taken to France for exchange and visited England where he was received at court and given a commission in the regular army. He returned to New Haven as a recruiting officer, retired on half-pay in 1748, and began a successful mercantile career. At the opening of the French and Indian War, Wooster was made colonel of a regiment sent to Crown Point where he served with distinction. Meanwhile, he had entered politics and served in the General Assembly as deputy from New Haven. At the news of Lexington and Concord, the doughty old fellow, now sixty-five years old, renounced his half-pay pension and sought a command of Connecticut militia. The General Assembly obliged and made him Major General of all the Connecticut forces, with Joseph Spencer, first Brigadier, and Israel Putnam, second Brigadier. This arrangement satisfied the traditional sense of order and hierarchy so natural to Connecticut politics, and no real problems seem to have occurred there. But when Congress took over the army, the whole order was unsettled.

Israel Putnam, as authentic a backwoods hero as Connecticut has ever provided, was a huge man of immense energies. He had unmatchable courage, legendary physical strength, and a degree of *sangfroid* at times of emergency that impressed some people as heartless. During the course of the war he had at least three men publicly executed for royalism and desertion, and once he paraded his troops past the corpse of one, while its clothes, which had been ignited from the barrels of the firing squad's guns, still burned. At Cambridge he was everywhere. Congress was especially impressed by a minor exploit involving the liberation of hundreds of hogs, sheep, and cows from a British-held island in Boston Harbor. Wooster, meanwhile, had remained in Connecticut, involved in planning and launching the Ticonderoga expedition and maintaining support for the New York patriots,* and Congress passed him over when handing out Continental Major-Generalships. There were to be four of these, and, of course, Artemas Ward, superseded by Washington, would get one. Another would go, on Washington's insistence, to the former professional British army officer, Charles Lee, who had been residing in Virginia since early in 1775. One each would be awarded to officers from New York and Connecticut. Philip Schuyler, an able veteral of colonial wars and present at Congress as a delegate from New York, got his colony's quota, "to Sweeten and to keep up the Spirit in that Province," as Dyer put it; and Putnam received Connecticut's. The outranked Wooster and Spencer were mortified.

Joseph Spencer, who had been Putnam's immediate superior, immediately left his troops at Roxbury to remonstrate with the Council of Safety at Lebanon. Samuel Huntington and William Williams were delegated to talk to Spencer and they spent all of one morning with him at Gray's Tavern. But it took a full Council meeting and the influence of Governor Trumbull to do the job. Spencer was finally persuaded to return to his command and serve under his younger, former-inferior officer. But his staff was not happy with the alteration, and forty-nine of his officers sent a remonstrance to the General Assembly protesting that the new organization "so far removes General

* Or rather attempting to draw the skittish New Yorkers into the action. Dyer wrote Governor Trumbull: ". . . it is apprehended still in New York (*i.e.*) their Cautious men are for saving for themselves and the Province a safe retreat if possoble [sic]. We readily see they most Carefully Avoid taking any h[an]d in these Matters, therefore the more they are brought to move and Apply the more they will Involve themselves in the same Predicament with the other Colonies, which will give us a stronger Security for their future firmness in the General Cause. . . ." As he said later, "about 12 hundred [troops] with Genll. Wooster are ordered to York for more reasons than one.

*Spencer* from his former command, that he cannot and will not continue in the service under this arrangement . . . we apprehend the morals and good order and discipline of our Troops will be greatly endangered under the present arrangement." The Assembly requested Governor Trumbull to write to Sherman, Dyer, and Deane, asking them to persuade the Congress "to devise some method of obviating the difficulties apprehended." At the same time, Trumbull was to write Spencer directly and "conjure him, by the love to his Country, to call to mind the constant and signal affection of his Country [Connecticut] to him . . . and request him not to precipitate a resolution to resign his command, and which will distress his Troops, and give great anxiety and dissatisfaction to his Country, which has placed, and continues to place high confidence in his wisdom, prudence, integrity, and military skill."

At Congress the delegation split. As might be expected, the youthful Deane supported the more aggressive Putnam, and damned slavish subservience to traditional seniority. Roger Sherman made a strong fight for his close New Haven friend Wooster, and Dyer also tried to persuade Congress to follow the order arranged by Connecticut. Deane, however, had no such objectives. After describing Wooster as an "old woman . . . unfit for a Major General of Connecticut forces . . .," he added, "As to *Spencer,* I once had a good opinion of him; but his leaving the forces in the manner I hear he has, shocks it very greatly, and if true, I wish him to resign at once and let another take his place. . . ." "Let it be remembered," he wrote later, "that [Putnam] had every vote of the Congress; and his health has been the second or third [toast] at almost all our tables in this city. . . ." Deane, declaring Wooster "totally unequal to the service," finally won Dyer over. Indeed, Dyer may not have been so eager to see Spencer stay in the service, for he wrote his wife that he regretted Spencer's lack of backbone, and had "designed to have taken his birth my self, as I believe I might [have] had the offer." He explained to Joseph Trumbull that Putnam's "Fame as a Warrior had been so far extended thro the Continent that it would be in Vain to urge any of our Genll officers in Competition with him and he Carried by Universal Voice." Sherman had to write his proud old friend, "Gen. Putnam's fame was spread abroad, and especially his successful enterprise at Noddle's Island, the account of which had just arrived, it gave him the preference in the opinion of the Delegates in general, so his appointment was unanimous among the colonies."

The matter, however, continued to heat relations among the three Connecticut delegates. "Pray listen to these reports" about the generals, Deane wrote to his wife, "and inform me how far I am charged with being active in this arrangement. I have various reasons to expect their friends [Wooster's and Spencer] will father it all on the old scape goat, as Sherman is known to favor Wooster, and Dyer and Spencer and brother Councilors." Later Deane told his wife that the attempts to prefer Wooster to Putnam were a "low, narrow, selfish, envious manoeuvre." "I see the bottom of the whole," he wrote, "and am well aware that the storm is raised, or at least blown up by others . . . but am determined to do my duty, and will on no occasion sacrifice the good of my country to the whim of any old man, or old woman rather, or their sticklers." Putnam, said Deane, "is not adept either at political or religious canting and cozening; he is no shake-hand body; he, therefore, is totally unfit for everything but fighting; *that* department, I never heard that these intriguing gentry wanted to interfere with him in." But if Putnam's promotion was not Deane's doing, then the crafty Wethersfield merchant was less than candid. He had recommended his stepson, Samuel Webb, to be Putnam's aide-de-camp and wrote Joseph Trumbull, "I have some little right to plead as I was the General's friend in the Assembly, & have not been idle here of which I make no merit, & only wish I may not be censured by certain persons."

For his part, Wooster declined a Continental brigadier's commission in favor of his command of the Connecticut militia, despite Sherman's attempts to reconcile the disappointed general to the lower rank. In March, 1777, another attempt to get a Continental commission for Wooster failed, but the effort would have been in vain. The brave David Wooster was mortally wounded in April as he led a harassing action on the rear of retreating Redcoats near the Tory-ridden town of Ridgefield. And so he died in his "bed of honor."

Connecticut's collection of Continental prizes included the Commissary Generalship which went to Joseph Trumbull, the Governor's son. Connecticut had been such a fruitful supplier of foodstuffs to the troops around Cambridge that it was natural for this important position to fall her way. Trumbull had a good friend at Congress in Deane, and Dyer was soon to be his father-in-law; and even Sherman, unlike his fellows, fully free of any taint of self interest, pushed for the young Lebanon merchant. The job was tremendously important, for surely the army would melt away if the soldiers went unfed, unclothed, and unarmed. It was also an exceptionally demanding task, requiring extraordinary energy, a quick improvising mind, and minute attention to detail. Trumbull was elected unanimously, and Deane happily wrote him the news, adding that it was "a post more lucrative than that of Secretary, but as you know, by experience, proportionately more fatiguing." And Dyer let Trumbull know that he hoped to get the wages "some raised." The Governor's younger son, John, was rewarded with the paymastership for the New York Department, at fifty dollars a month, thirty less than Joseph's "more lucrative" salary.

But by now the delegates were getting tired. Roger Sherman

wrote his good, old friend William Williams that he "had but little lesure being obliged to attend Congress from eight or nine in the morning to four or five in the afternoon . . . It has been very tedious sitting here this hot season," he added, and "I have not been absent at any time while Congress has been sitting." The delegates still hoped that the next session of Congress would be held in Hartford, but not too soon. "We are all exhausted sitting so long at this place," wrote Dyer, "and being so long confined together that we feel pretty much as a Number of passangers confined together on board ship in a long voyage." "The Congress," reported Silas Deane tersely, "have now sat, without a day's respite since the 10th of May, and consequently are much fatigued." With relief the body adjourned on August 2, 1775, to reconvene on September 12.

For the Connecticut delegates, this trip home was even more comfortable than previous ones, because Deane had had his carriage made over into a phaeton. The alteration was made necessary by the apparent carelessness of Sherman, who had borrowed the chaise two weeks earlier and "had it broke intirely." Deane wrote his wife about this: "I lent my chaise to Mr. Sherman yesterday and it is broke to pieces; but shall repair it, I believe, by a new one for the old one is totally broke and destroyed." "I hope," he confided to his wife three days later, "to be home in three weeks if I get my carriage repaired in season; it must be made, in a manner, new. Mr. Sherman is, I think peculiarly unfortunate, at Philadelphia, tho' by no means faulty." But such is the ability of politicians to cover their personal animosities that the trio was able to travel together for the five-day ride home, sharing expenses as they went.

## Politics and Preludes

WITH its right arm, Congress prepared for war, with its left, it offered the mother country a sort of half-hearted handshake. The radicals, trying so hard to stand up straight that they almost fell over backward, permitted their more timorous colleagues to write and send to England a conciliatory offering, the so-called Olive Branch Petition, adopted on July 5, 1775. The Petition, addressed to the "Most Gracious Sovereign," from "your Majesty's faithful subjects," outlined the wonderful mutual advantages of the old imperial connection, emphasized the cooperation among all its parts during the French and Indian

29

War, and then noted the new Parliamentary acts "that filled their minds with the most painful fears, . . . of a foreign quarrel quickly succeeded by domestick danger . . . of a more dreadful kind." It was no fault of the King, however, only that of "Your Majesty's Ministers" who were guilty of "delusive preferences, fruitless terrours, and unavailing severities." Protesting attachment to "your Majesty's person, family, and Government, with all devotion that principle and affection can inspire," the Petition went on to beseech the King "to procure us relief from our afflicting fears and jealousies . . . to settle peace through every part of our Dominions."

Roger Sherman sang the tune more in Connecticut's key when he wrote that "The Congress are very diligent in making every needful provision in their power for the Support of the American Cause at the same time do not neglect any probable means of a reconciliation with Great Britain, tho' I have no expectation that administration will be reconciled unless the Colonies submit to their Arbitrary system, or convince them that it is not in their power to carry it into execution." Eliphalet Dyer thought John Dickinson, the Petition's penman, "not very highly Esteemed in Congress," a view more pungently expressed by John Adams who referred to Dickinson as a "piddling Genius" whose work had "given a silly Cast to our whole Doings."

Much more to the liking of Connecticut's Continental delegates than the Olive Branch Petition, was a second document drawn up and adopted in the last hot weeks of the Philadelphia session. This was the famous "Declaration . . . setting forth the causes and necessity of their taking up Arms." Government, the Declaration pointed out, exists solely to promote the welfare of mankind, but Parliament, "stimulated by an inordinate passion for a power" known to be unconstitutional, have "attempted to effect their cruel and impolitick purpose of enslaving these Colonies by violence, and have thereby rendered it necessary for us to close with their last appeal from reason to arms." Congress protested its moderation, but Gage had "butchered our countrymen"; Carleton was "instigating . . . the Indians to fall upon us"; and ahead lay only "the complicated calamities of fire, sword and famine." Only resistance was left. "Our cause is just. Our union is perfect. Our internal resources are great . . . we will, in defiance of every hazard [employ our energy, arms and faith] . . . being; with one mind, resolved to die freemen rather than live slaves." The King, of course, deliberately and with malice aforethought, maintained the strictest and most insulting ignorance of the documents when they arrived before his Council.

The Connecticut delegates were not surprised at the King's action, and, with more at stake than most others, they were ready to move ahead. Once Patrick Henry asked Roger Sherman why Connecticuters were so much more ardent in the cause of liberty than others. Sherman replied, "Because we have more to lose, sir—our precious Charter." It had always been held hostage to Connecticut's good behavior, and at least one attempt to take it away was barely foiled. Now Connecticut leaders were tired of walking the tightrope. "I want to know what measures the ministry will take after hearing of the Battle of Concord and Lexington," Sherman wrote impatiently; "if they don't relax, but order reinforcements, I hope every Colony will take Government fully into their own hands until matters are settled."

Feisty Eliphalet Dyer had been on edge for over a decade. Even before the passage of the Stamp Act of 1765 he saw the handwriting on the wall. In 1764 he suggested to Governor Fitch that in view of British policy, the colonies "may for the future, bid Farewell to Freedom and Liberty, burn their Charters, and make the best of Thraldom and Slavery." In the decade that had passed, British measures had fulfilled his worst nightmares, but had turned his head toward "Freedom and Liberty," with no longer any thought of burning charters. Dyer was so much associated with the independence movement that he was assigned to the Assembly committee directed to write a resolution urging Congress to declare itself on the matter.

In May, 1775, the Connecticut Assembly drew up a complete list of the rights of the colonists and the abuses of Parliament. The rights abused are those of taxation, local jury trials, local control of judges, interference with commerce, the establishment of Roman Catholicism in Quebec, "a tyranny erected . . . to the great danger of neighboring colonies." Finally, the Assembly pointed out that "fleets and armies have been sent into a neighboring Colony to force them to submit to slavery and awe the other Colonies to submission by the example of vengeance inflicted on her, who have, besides the usual calamities and insults that proceed from standing armies, fortified the town of Boston, driven the peaceable inhabitants from their dwellings, and inbrued their hands in the blood of our countrymen. . . ." Worse still than the specific calamities of the case was the general degradation that Parliamentary ministers would bring to America. "Religion, property, personal safety, learning, arts, public and private virtue, social happiness and every blessing attendant on liberty will fall victims to the principles and measures advanced and pursued against us, whilst shameless vice, infidelity, irreligion, abject dependence, ignorance, superstition, meanness, servility and the whole train of despotism, present themselves to our view in melancholy prospect." The Assembly would grant Parliament, at this point, the right to regulate Connecticut's external commerce, desiring only "to preserve their antient constitution as it has been understood and practised upon from the beginning."

In the midst of these constitutional and propagandistic developments, the General Assembly changed its delegation to Congress. On November 3, 1774, the Council of Safety had reappointed Deane,

Dyer, and Sherman, and appointed Titus Hosmer and Jonathan Sturges as well, neither of whom attended in 1775 or 1776. But a year later, as a step in the direction of articulating her relationship with the United Colonies, the Assembly in October, 1775, took the election of delegates upon itself. On October 12, it reelected Sherman and Hosmer and elected Oliver Wolcott, Samuel Huntington, and William Williams. Sherman, Wolcott, and Huntington were the three with the highest vote and so were authorized to attend "for the year ensuing," with Hosmer and Williams "filling-in" in case of sickness or absence for any other reason. The new delegation was to take its seats as soon in January as Congress adjourned, and they arrived there on the 16th.

About half of the May, 1775, deputies were replaced in October, not an especially high rate of turnover, but a Deane correspondent saw in the elections a plot to unseat the energetic delegate. The "Junto," wrote Thomas Mumford, "had levied their artilery strongly fortified against you," and caused the defeat of pro-Deane deputies. The "Junto" was made up of William Williams, who got himself elected both to Congress and as Speaker of the Connecticut House; and Sherman's New Haven friends who caballed at Stephen Munson's tavern, next to Sherman's house near the Green. Deane knew that Williams was in on it. It was, he said, that "rascally junto . . . those party people . . . agitated and stirred on by that little malevolent prig in buckram." As for "my old colleage Sh----n," Deane carped later to his wife, "suffice it to say, that if the order of the Jesuits is extinct their practices are not out of fashion, even among modern New Light Saints. . . ."

From the start, Deane had not been trusted by some of his fellow politicians. William Williams had feared that Deane might use the public business to further his own private interests, and there is evidence to support his suspicion. Deane was deeply involved with New York and Philadelphia merchants, most of whom were aligned with the conservatives in Congress. In particular, he was associated with Robert Morris in very large-scale, transatlantic, commercial ventures, and with Samuel Warton of Philadelphia. In the latter connection, he was involved with his secretary Edward Bancroft, a successful British spy, in a dubious insurance scheme in which Deane's access to confidential information played a central part. Little of this, if any, was known to Deane's enemies in Connecticut, but their suspicions were high.

The elections to the Assembly in October, 1775, boded ill for him, and perhaps he suspected it. "I suppose Connecticut politicians have been busy," he wrote, "and that the Nomination will be varied, but I hope not very greatly, as I wish for the old steady plan of the Colony, in preference to any private view, either for myself or friends." In addition to Deane's insufficiency of Puritan rectitude, he had also antagonized the Susquehanna faction. The activities of the Connecticut settlers in the Wyoming Valley of Pennsylvania were causing the delegation at Philadelphia acute embarrassment. In May, 1774, the General Assembly had assumed jurisdiction over the Susquehanna Company's claim of about one-third of the colony of Pennsylvania, land claimed also by the Pennsylvania proprietors. Connecticut established the town of Westmoreland there and incorporated it into her colony government. Already this was beginning to upset inter-colonial relations, and to cause some hard feelings between the delegates from Pennsylvania and their colleagues from Connecticut. At the end of the first Congressional session, the Pennsylvanians had asked the Yankees to calm down their obstreperous western appendage in the Wyoming Valley, and Dyer, Deane, and Sherman wrote to the western leader "that there is great danger of discord and Contention if not Hostility & bloodshed between the People setling under Connecticut Claim & those under Pensylvania which would be attended with the most unhappy consequences at this time of general Calamity & when we want our whole United Strength [against] our common enemy." But the frontier continued in ferment, and Pennsylvania submitted a resolution laying the "Connecticut Intrusion before Congress that something be done to quiet their minds." But the issue was not clear; one Pennsylvanian, Thomas Willing, indicated that there were two sides to the question, and suggested the need of an umpire. Sherman, taking advantage of the opening, said that he thought agreement might be made on a temporary line of separation. But Dyer was the major *bête noire* of the Pennsylvania landholders, waxing so hot that he ultimately destroyed his effectiveness in the issue. Deane, courting the favor of powerful Pennsylvania commercial interests, had opposed the Connecticut settlers, calling their activities a "mad frolic."

Deane was putting American, as well as his own, interests above those of Connecticut. He thought that "the indiscreet zeal of Col. Dyer did the Cause no service and . . . much hurt himself among the people of influence . . . the Col. meant well, but disputing on the Connecticut claim in all Companies . . . served to increase and inflame the Apprehensions of The people. Mr. Sherman and myself pursued quite a different plan for my own part, I avoided the dispute wholly and when forced upon it expressed my warmest wishes for a friendly Settlement. By this means I stood well with The more dispassionate of the other party. . . ." Deane's weaseling however, caused him to stand very badly with the Susquehannah party in Connecticut—long his principal support—and he lost his seat in the election underway at the very moment he penned these words.

Dyer, too, had antagonized his stalwarts by his ineffective efforts on behalf of the Company. It is ironic that the two major Susquehannah promoters should be done in by the cause they thought they could

33

protect by going to Philadelphia in the first place. On January 16, 1776, when Samuel Huntington and Oliver Wolcott arrived to replace their defeated colleagues, Dyer wrote to Joseph Trumbull that he was "happily relieved in a most important critical situation of Congress." He remained until the 20th, when Deane reported that Dyer had "set off in a violent hurry." Deane also pretended satisfaction at his release from duty: "I have not sat in Congress since last Tuesday, when, with pleasure, I gave place to my successor, of whom . . . I say nothing." Dyer, however, reported Deane as "confoundedly Chagrined at his recall," and a couple of years later Deane admitted that "I will confess to you that I was hurt in the manner in which I was dismissed from being a delegate."

## The Great Declaration

THE Signers of the Declaration of Independence are America's nearest approximation to national saints. Dyer and Deane, then, whisked off the stage at the moment that immortality was framed, gave their places not just then, but forever, to Samuel Huntington, Oliver Wolcott, and William Williams. Huntington, in particular, became a major Congressional figure.

Samuel Huntington, a self-taught lawyer, moved from his native Windham to Norwich in 1760. An early radical, he was sent to the General Assembly in 1765, the year of the Stamp Act, and he worked his way up to the Council ten years later. Huntington was first elected to Congress in October, 1775, and was thereafter annually elected until 1784, when the three-year term became effective. Thus, his Council and Congressional careers were concurrent. Except for 1777 and 1782, he was at Congress about six months out of every year between 1775 and 1784. On September 28, 1779, he was elected President of the Congress to replace John Jay who had been commissioned to negotiate a treaty with Spain. Huntington held this post until July, 1781, when ill health forced his resignation. No doubt his personal political philosophy worked well. "I find one Consolation very necessary in public life," he wrote a young friend and future governor, "that is to believe or act as if I did fully believe there are many wise men who can Judge better then myself on Important subjects, and I have the happiness generally to unite in promoting their determinations, as far as duty requires in any Sphere I am called to act in."

Huntington was reserved—even cold—in public, and parsimonious to a degree unusual even in Calvinist Connecticut. But among his small group of cronies he was good,—though teetotaling—company. "We have been uncommonly dull this summer," he wrote a friend in 1785. "I have studied much, learnt little, wrote ad infinitum. Come down you Dog and make us merry; for our Lads are void of spirit, and our Girls are full of Spunk. . . ." Huntington was elected lieutenant governor in 1784, and two years later he succeeded to the gubernatorial chair, a seat he held till his death in 1796. But his private playfulness was not inhibited by the new honor. "My horse is not a good trooper," he wrote his best friend the fall after his election, "he started upon me this Day, & tore a hole thro' my foot, boot, stocking & all. . . . I am reduced by the accident above cited, to the deplorable necessity of sitting Day unto Day, & night unto night, with my bow in one hand, violin in the other—& drawing the Rock and &c after me, as old Mr. Orpheus used to do; I have not yet got so expert as to draw a Wife as the afore'd Orpheus did, & if I should, I do not wish to draw from her the same place as we have hot Women enough here. . . ." His private character, however playful, was still abstemious and even miserly. He died in January, 1796, and a hostile commentator described the funeral.

> A mistake was made. . .in not putting the Gov's sword onto his coffin; but as Excellency commonly wore a borro'd sword, I think the omission was very proper. Another mistake was discovered by the soldiers, they had not the offer of anything to drink, but as this was perfectly conformable to his Excellency's practice while living, this must be excused— No one can expect a dead man to do things inconsistent with his living principles.

Oliver Wolcott, the third of Connecticut's "Signers," was one of Governor Roger Wolcott's fourteen children. He was graduated from Yale, and when Litchfield County was organized in 1751, his father appointed him sheriff there, though he was only then twenty-five years old. This was the beginning of the smooth upward climb in public office almost guaranteed to the sons of Connecticut's inner circle. He thenceforth devoted himself to his Litchfield lands and farms and to his public career and duties. Wolcott served in the House, and in 1771 was elected to the Council. Ultimately, he became lieutenant governor, an office he held for ten years until Samuel Huntington's death in 1796 gave him the gubernatorial chair.

Every year from 1775 through the war's end in 1783, Wolcott was elected a delegate to Congress. He attended, all told, about thirty-one months during that time. In addition, he carried out a number of missions to Indian tribes in upstate New York, and, in fact, made Indian affairs something of a specialty.

A couple of weeks after his first arrival at Philadelphia, he wrote, "If you should ask me how I like attending Congress, I must tell you I cannot answer that question yet. I hope I shall do my duty, and have satisfaction in doing it." When the British threatened Philadelphia, he wrote to a troubled wife, "My Dear . . . the Congress . . . have adjourned themselves to Baltimore in Maryland, a Place about 110 miles from this City, as it was judged that the Council of America ought not to Sit in a Place liable to be interrupted, by the rude Disorder of Arms. . . ." Baltimore he found unobjectionable except that it was "too distant from my Friends, and is too dirty and too dear." And York, where Congress later itinerated, Wolcott found "much more pleasant than Baltimore but publick and private Virtue I suppose is much the same here as there." He was staying at a public house, but looking for private lodgings, though, he wrote his wife, "I understand that a single Man exclusive of Horskeeping cannot probably live under at least ten pounds per Week. Everything here bears an enormous price."

It was Wolcott's practice to attend Congress for about six months a year, a fair arrangement, since seven delegates were elected annually, but only three were to attend at a time. After the first three years, he began to cut this down to three, two, and even one-month stints. By April, 1778, he was numbering the days till his "half year's Service counting to next Novr" would end. "The Service in attending Congress is more arduous than I had before known it. . . . At present I am not so well as to attend. . . ." When the war was over he never went again.

William Williams was Connecticut's fourth "Signer." Williams was not present to debate the Declaration, but arrived in Philadelphia in time to put his name to it. He was a Harvard graduate, but retained throughout his long life the same commitment to primative Calvinism as his self-educated colleagues, Sherman and Huntington. He was born in 1731, the same year as Huntington, the son of Solomon Williams, Lebanon's minister, and in 1771 married Mary, a daughter of Governor Jonathan Trumbull. Williams went on the disastrous Lake George campaign in 1775 under a cousin, Colonel Ephraim Williams, who died in the battle. This unfortunate event, coupled with his experience with the British regulars, whose "haughtiness, and arbitary conduct, and . . . inattention to the interests of America," disgusted him. He became convinced, according to an early biographer, that the prosperity and well-being of Americans would never be safe except under their own government. After studying theology briefly, he became a merchant, in which his Trumbull connection no doubt proved useful.

Williams was the principal figure in Lebanon government: he was town clerk almost all of the years between 1752 and 1802 and selectman for twenty-five years after 1760. In 1757 he began a career in the General Assembly where he sat for ninety consecutive sessions, interrupted only by his attendance at the Continental Congress. In the political upset of 1766 he became clerk of the House, and took an active part in the opposition to the Stamp Act and Townshend acts, referring to England as America's "Step Mother country." After the Boston Massacre he wrote that the British ministry "seem to have forgotten her relation; and prefer the hazard of obtaining from us the forced and unnatural submission of slaves." He was an original member of the Connecticut Committee of Safety, and as early as July, 1774, urged his countrymen to "take up arms and shed rivers of Blood in defence of our almost infinitely important Cause." As clerk to the Council of Safety, which met in Lebanon at his father-in-law the governor's office, Williams attended almost all of the 1,145 sessions.

Williams was of the Calvinist group of Connecticut and Continental politicians. "God has most certainly a controversy with this people," he wrote, "and he is most certainly able to manage it, and he will accomplish his designs, and bring us to repentance and reformation or destroy us." He hated frivolous celebration and any sort of secular pomp or festivity. He was annoyed by celebrations of the Fourth of July in Philadelphia, and later, when the British occupied the city, he wrote, "I expected from the former conduct of Providence toward us since the beginning of this Contest, That Philadelphia so much the Mistress of Iniquity would be taken, and Corrected; and that this event will finally prove the Overthrow of the Enemy—However God is righteous—and His ways tho' dark and intricate to us, yet they are just and faithful—."

He was much disliked by the Deane coterie, and his Trumbull brothers-in-law. Regarding Williams' replacement of Deane at Congress, John Trumbull, the "Connecticut Wit" and a distant cousin, later wrote:

> A man of Congress asked thus
>   "How comes it, Poet Tombel,
> Your State doth send a Fool to us
>   Whose Name is William Wimble"?
> The Poet did this Speech relate,
>   "From honest views we sent him.
> The Fools are many in our State,
>   He goes to represent 'em."

Williams was uncomfortable outside Connecticut. He shared the simple provincialism of Sherman and Huntington, and he refused public appointments that would take him away from his beloved home on the Lebanon green. Though elected to Congress five times, he served only two terms totalling eight months.

Huntington, Sherman, and Wolcott were at Philadelphia for the great debate on Independence, well primed by the statements of principle and policy passed by the Connecticut Assembly. The Assembly adjourned its regular, but especially long, May session on June 8. But no sooner was that done than the Governor received word of Richard Henry Lee's resolution for independence which was before Congress from June 7, 1776, till its passage on July 2. Certainly the delegation needed no instructions, but the Governor called the excited and eager deputies back into special session on June 14, to make explicit what the leadership already knew. The next morning the House unanimously approved a resolution confirmed by the Council in the afternoon.

The Assembly, in view of the many acts of Parliament "subversive of the antient just and constitutional rights of this and the rest of the English Colonies in America," instructed the delegates at Congress "to propose to that respectable body, to declare the United American Colonies Free and Independent States. . . ." This resolution was similar to instructions from other colonies, most of whom copied from those of Virginia; but the long self-governing Connecticut Assembly considered any mention of Parliament irrelevent and called for a renunciation of "all allegiance to the King of Great Britain" only. In addition, the delegates were instructed to assent to measures "for forming foreign alliances, or any plan of operation for necessary and mutual defence." Connecticut went beyond the other colonies in suggesting "a regular and permanent Plan of Union and Confederation of the Colonies, for the security and preservation of their just rights and liberties and for mutual defence and security. . . ."

In keeping with the Colony's Calvinist world view, Governor Trumbull, like so many Americans after him, saw the whole course of events that would culminate in "Independency" as part of God's Design. The liberty of the people was His desire, but "moral Evil" had been introduced and "Vice and Iniquity came in like a Flood, and Mankind became exposed, and a prey to the Violence, Injustice and Oppression of one another." An unnatural King was "extirpating the Rights of *America*," but with God's help and that of "upwards of Seven Thousand able and effective Men," with "large and liberal Pay and Encouragements," the tyrant could be defeated. "The Cause is certainly a just and all glorious one," Trumbull concluded, "God is able to save us in such way and Manner as he pleases, and to humble our proud Oppressors."

The Assembly's instructions would have reached Philadelphia not later than June 20, and perhaps a day or two earlier. But the delegates had no need of them to read the Connecticut mind. On the very day the Assembly sent them down, Wolcott wrote his wife that "we seem at present to be in the Midst of a great Revolution, which will probably be attended with most important Consequences. Every Thing is leading to the lasting Independence of these Colonies. . . ."

38

A declaration of independence had been in the minds of radical Congressmen for many months, but there was enough conservative sentiment still among Pennsylvanians, New Yorkers, and others from the middle colonies, to delay an open and explicit debate. That came, however, in the days after June 7 with Richard Henry Lee's resolution "That these United Colonies are, and of right ought to be, free and independent States. . . ." Dyer and Deane had been replaced on January 16 by Samuel Huntington and Oliver Wolcott, but these two men were no less Whiggish than their predecessors; and of course Roger Sherman, home for a visit, came back in April.

Indeed, when on June 11 a committee to prepare the declaration was established, Sherman was included, along with Jefferson, Adams, Franklin, and the timorous Robert Livingston. The conservative element managed to postpone a vote until July 2; meanwhile, the official instructions from the Connecticut General Assembly arrived in Philadelphia about June 20. As the month wore on, instructions from other colonies arrived, but South Carolina, Pennsylvania, Delaware, and New York held out even as late as July 1. On July 2, however, a number of opposition figures deliberately absented themselves, the New York delegation remained silent, and new members from Pennsylvania and Delaware arrived. Thus, it was possible on that day to achieve a vote for independence, which, if not exactly unanimous, at least had no states in the negative.

The draft Declaration was reported out of committee on June 28 and was thus under discussion before the July 2 vote. That document is almost entirely the work of Thomas Jefferson, though Congress cut about a quarter of his draft, and altered his phrases in many instances. Franklin and Adams made some minor changes before it came before the whole body, but apparently Jefferson didn't even show it to either Sherman or Livingston.

There is no doubt that the Connecticut delegates supported the Declaration, though no evidence of their part, if any, in the debate remains. Wolcott became ill, "owing," he supposed, "to a too long confined way of living," and he left Philadelphia about June 28. But Sherman and Huntington voted "aye" on July 2 for Lee's resolution, and again on July 4 for the revised Declaration. On that day, Congress ordered that copies of the document be printed and transmitted to the colonies—shortly to be states. New York's adherence to the Declaration was certified on the 15th, and the statement of unanimity was now accurate. On July 19, Congress resolved that the Declaration be engrossed on parchment, and the title was officially attached to it at that time. Then, on August 2, the parchment copy was signed by those members then in attendance. From Connecticut they were Roger Sherman, Samuel Huntington, and William Williams, who had been dispatched by the Council of Safety to replace Wolcott and arrived in Philadelphia about July 29. Wolcott returned about October 1 and signed the parchment copy at that time.

On July 5 or 6, President John Hancock transmitted paper copies of the Declaration to each of the colonies, but Connecticut's Council of Safety first received its copy in a letter from Joseph Trumbull to William Williams that arrived in Lebanon on Thursday, July 11. The Council, on Friday, took up the matter of publishing the Declaration to the public, but "concluded to lay it by for the present." Finally on July 18, the Council decided to "let the matter of publishing the Independency remain for the determination of the General Assembly at their next stated session." Actually, however, there was no need for official haste. The editors of the *Connecticut Journal* had the text of the Declaration on July 10, and interested citizens could buy copies at the *Journal* office in Hartford the next day. As its first action of the October, 1776, session the General Assembly resolved, quoting the Lee resolution almost verbatim, "That they approve the Declaration of Independence published by said Congress, and that this Colony is and of right ought to be a free and independent State, and that the inhabitants thereof are absolved from all allegiance to the British Crown and all political connection between them and the King of Great Britain is, and ought to be, totally dissolved." An authenticated copy with the "names of the Members of Congress subscribing the same" was sent to each state by Congressional order of January 18, 1777, and the General Assembly recorded it in August.

# Affairs, Foreign and Domestic

As boys will be boys, so politicians will be politicians. As God helps those who help themselves, a call to public office is inevitably an echo of an aspirant's offer. Indeed, it was a fundamental truism of Enlightenment America that the public welfare is best promoted when it coincides with the self-interest of its promoters. Roger Sherman, for instance, was fond of quoting Alexander Pope: "Reason and passion answer one great Aim," he wrote in one of a series of almanacs he published in the 1750's, "And true self love and social are the same." For Sherman, and for the other secular Calvinists like Huntington and Williams, this meant that self-interest was so tied up with the well-being of society that, in a republican society, selfishness would be willfully subordinated to the general welfare. Indeed, selfishness and sin, and social consciousness and virtue, became almost synonymous.

An alteration of words, however, could justify the satisfaction of private desires through the state; but there is a great difference between "what's good for me is good for society," and "what's good for society is good for me." One of the major differences that developed in the Continental Congress in the mid-1770's grew out of these different perspectives. Though the Connecticut delegation was profoundly Calvinist and social for the most part, there was a very active individual fly in the ointment. His name was Silas Deane.

Deane entered politics upon the death of his first wife, and was elected deputy from Wethersfield in 1765, an office he maintained until 1775 when he was away at Congress. He was a member of the original Council of Safety which in 1773 was called the Committee of Correspondence. Always a promoter, he held speculative interests in Susquehanna lands, and may have held some in Vermont as well. Thus he was much interested in launching the Ticonderoga expedition and in securing a strong Susquehanna delegation to go to Congress in 1774.

Without in any way belittling Deane's commitment to American independence, it is certainly true that he saw the contest also as a wonderful mercantile opportunity for himself and his friends. His Calvinist colleagues suspected that this was the case, and they seem to have reacted violently to any indication of a self-interested motive. Sherman, Huntington, Dyer, and others all gave up good mercantile and law practices to serve in the cause, and they were losing money fast. The eighteen shillings a day paid for their services hardly covered expenses at Philadelphia, and, furthermore, payments were frequently delayed for years. They were not about to let too aggressive, high-flown young Deane—sixteen years younger than Dyer and Sherman—grab off plums that they were unwilling to pick themselves.

Sherman—with Samuel Adams the most Calvinist of the Calvinist wing of Congress—really raised Deane's hackles. There is no doubt that Sherman was a prudish nuisance, and that his correct conduct brought out Deane's fundamental New England guilt. At Philadelphia, Deane found an affinity with the more high-toned delegates from the middle states, and lent himself to their efforts to cast the Congress in a conservative mold. This might appear strange, for Deane had shone as one of the hottest of independence men. But he could perceive who was going to butter the Continental bread, and he wanted to be on the right side. Deane even cast aside his Susquehannah obligations in his courtship of Robert Morris and the great Philadelphia commercial magnates. His general "un-Connecticut" attitude, the abandonment of the Susquehannah constituency, and the manipulations of his suspicious colleagues caused his dismissal from the delegation in 1775 as has been described.

Deane's great ability and energy were not to be dispensed with, however, and two secret Congressional committees were determined to put them to work. One of these was known simply as the Secret Committee, and by it Deane was commissioned to secure supplies abroad—but surreptitiously. The other, the Committee of Secret Correspondence, sent him to France to attempt to secure an alliance or secret understanding from the foreign minister, Count Vergennes. John Adams thought that the commissions were created especially for Deane, and even at his solicitation. Indeed, wrote a Massachusetts colleague, "If Silas and his york connections could have a good opening to transfer their whole property to the other side of the water it is not impossible that they would *gladly* do it." Deane himself wrote glowingly to a connection at home: "The Congress have also appointed a Secret Committee for Supplying the Continent with certain Necessary Articles. of this I am one, and wish I could see you, or some other of my Connecticut Mercantile Friends here, as it would be in my power to help them, and in theirs to serve their Country. this hi[nt is a]ll I can give on this head, and if you will come down, the sooner the better."

It was in France that the fun began, because, once there, Deane would be competing for influence with one Arthur Lee, brilliant, European-educated scholar, lawyer, and physician, brother of Francis Lightfoot and Richard Henry Lee, both important Congressional figures. Lee saw himself as America's principal propagandist and agent in Europe, and he resented Deane's activities there. The pair of them were associated with Benjamin Franklin in 1776 as agents to seek French financial aid. Lee was almost paranoid in his suspicions of Deane, and Deane did not like one bit the idea of anyone looking over his shoulder while juggling private and public accounts in Paris. Congress, already somewhat divided over the questions of independence and military appointments, became visibly factionalized over the Deane-Lee imbroglio.

The matter simmered and bubbled as Deane got cozy with the French, who began sending droves of their younger sons to Congress for commissions in the Continental Army—where they ran into competition with good Americans on the spot. Dyer, back in Congress in July of '77, wrote Deane's good friend Joseph Trumbull about this business. "This is a most unhappy affair and our old Friend D[e]an has been in more Instances than one, Imprudent to the last degree he has brot us into the most unhappy Dilemna in several of his Contracts and Stipulations with Gentn sending over Swarms of Commanders Pensioners etc." Congress, he concluded, was "embarrassed and plagued with D-ns Imprudence." Deane's conduct was no surprise to some: a Massachusetts delegate wrote, "I have but a poor Idea of that Gentleman's ability to guard against french finess and flattery."

42

Then the anti-Deane forces got a handy handle to grab when Lee claimed that the French provisions for which Deane was billing Congress were actually gifts from the French government.

William Williams, now at Congress, described the whole affair to Roger Sherman sitting with the Council of Safety in Connecticut. Sherman's deep suspicions—by now convictions—of Deane's lack of virtue were inflamed. "If the Gentleman you mention went to such lengths, without authority," worried Sherman, "what may be expected when he has plenary power to bind in all cases—To make the matter more easy he might be Sent for, to give more full intelligence than can be communicated by writing." The deft old cobbler knew also how to wield a scalpel. Sherman's good friend Sam Adams, in reference to Deane, had written, that "a Monopoly of Trade, and not the Liberty of their Country, is the sole Object of some Men's Views." Lee, writing from France, and Adams, Sherman, and others at Congress were then able to convince that body to recall the Wethersfield merchant. This was done in the autumn of '77, but Deane delayed, waiting to sign the treaties with France and frantically trying to get his accounts in order. He was kept informed by his friend, Connecticut delegate Titus Hosmer, an exact contemporary who was graduated from Yale the year before Deane.

Titus Hosmer was on his way to becoming one of the young, progressive nationalists who came to dominate Connecticut politics in the late 1780's. He was elected to Congress every year but 1776 until his early death in 1780. However, he did not attend until Deane was in trouble, and then went only for the period of his friend's interrogation, the summer of 1778. He was dismayed at the treatment Deane received, and also shocked at the dalliance of Congress in general. He wrote:

> The Southern States are fixed against holding Congress more than once a day; our hours are fixed from nine in the forenoon to two in the afternoon. If these were punctually attended it would be perhaps as much as could be spared from committees, other business which must be done out of Congress hours. Nine States make a Congress [quorum], some States have delegates so very negligent, so much immersed in the pursuit of pleasure or [private] business, that it is very rare we can make a Congress before near eleven o'clock, . . . . When we are assembled several gentlemen have such a knack at starting questions of order, raising debates upon critical, captious, and trifling amendments, protracting them by long speeches, by postponing, calling for the previous question, and other arts, that it is almost impossible to get an important question decided at one sitting; and if it is put over to another day, the field is open to be gone over again, precious time is lost, and the public business left undone.

Much of the delay was intentional, which Hosmer, no doubt, realized. There was no real desire by either faction in Congress to air the Deane accounts. Hosmer told Deane that it was the aim of a small group of Lee partisans to wear him down with delays and petty harrassments. Deane knew it, too, and he poured out his frustrations in a letter to John Hancock: ". . . you are not a Stranger to what a certain Triumvirate, who have been from the first members of Congress are equall. The baseness and ingratitude of one of them [S. Adams] you have sufficiently experienced in private Life, to know him capable of anything in public; and my old colleague Roger [Sherman], the Jesuit, with their Southern associate [R. H. Lee], have been indefatigable ever since my Arrival. Roger, indeed, is at present on a Tour of the Army, and thence to New Haven, to stir up the minds of the Faithful there against the next Election of Delegates; he is expected back in a few Days, when perhaps they will be ready to take the Field. . . ."

But there were delays and more delays. Finally in September, Deane was told to commit his report to writing, and then in December he was permitted to read most of it to Congress. On the last day of 1778, Deane was informed that Congress would let him know "their future orders." Many months later he received his "orders," and they were that he leave America only with permission of Congress. Two years later he was permitted to depart, and went back to France to see if he could get his accounts straightened out. This he was unable to do, and, losing confidence in himself and the American cause, he wrote letters home urging reconcilation with England and an end to the war. The letters were intercepted and printed in Loyalist newspapers. For Deane, there was no possibility of returning now, and he stayed in exile until 1789, when, on his much-delayed return, he died on a ship at sea.

Another element of the Deane-Lee fight was the dichotomous affinities that were developing in Congress between the Francophobes and the Francophiles. There is a fair degree of coincidence of New England Calvinist, radical purist, and anti-French sentiment. It is natural that the old Congregationalists would be distrustful of Papist France, but, in addition, that nation was working hard to minimize American claims to fishing rights off the coasts of North America. This issue divided New Englanders from middle and southern state delegates, and strengthened the factions that were developing so rapidly and profoundly in the late seventies. The French minister to Congress, Gerard, used this split to foster distrust of Lee, who, though a Virginian, was part of the radical New England faction; and to strengthen the hand of Deane, who, though a New Englander, was a member of the middle states conservative faction. The division deepened on the question of whom to appoint to negotiate the treaties with France and Spain. The radicals fought to keep Lee in Spain, but they were even more determined to send a New Englander to negotiate with France where the fisheries question would arise. As a com-

promise, in a series of bitterly-fought votes in September, 1779, the
radicals, although forced to give up Lee in favor of John Jay, got John
Adams appointed to negotiate with the French.

In general, the radicals wanted to keep their revolution pure and
to depend on as little foreign aid as possible. Roger Sherman, in 1775,
had noted that among "the great principles of alliance the only effective one is a right resulting from a firm and dignified national courage
to ask other powers to become sharers in our Strength, and not part-
ners in our weakness. . . . The more attention we pay to our own resources and the less we rely upon others, the more Surely Shall we
provide for our own honor and Success, and retrieve that balance between the contending European powers. . . ." A foreign loan, he said
in 1779, "I should not be very fond of if we can do without it." Four
years later, Oliver Ellsworth was of the same mind. Making virtue out
of necessity on the failure of Congress to secure a foreign loan, he
wrote that no disappointment ought arise. "We are now reduced to the
necessity of taxing ourselves and paying as we go; which though more
irksome for the present, may be less so hereafter than a foreign debt
and less dangerous to the liberties of the people."

Dislike it as they might, foreign aid was essential; ministers *did*
have to be appointed, commercial and military treaties negotiated, and
loans arranged. Convinced finally that they could not go it alone,
the radicals wanted to control matters as much as possible. To this effect, they tried to keep up their representation in Congress and to
maintain some continuity within it. When Deane arrived back in
Philadelphia, he exposed the whole radical caucus in an article published in papers throughout the states under the pseudonym, "O Tem-
pore! O Mores!" Oliver Ellsworth strove to vitiate the Deane accusa-
tions in his own newspaper letters, but his response is not nearly so
convincing as Deane's charges.

Factions were present in Connecticut, too; and there the older,
Calvinist group was in full control. Deane was abroad or neutralized
in Philadelphia in 1779–1780, and then in bitter exile in England.
Joseph Trumbull died in 1778, as did Hosmer two years later. Jesse
Root, who was a friend of Deane's and shared the high nationalism of
that circle, hung on, as did Benjamin Huntington, but the impelling
force of the young mercantile nationalists was slowed if not tempo-
rarily halted, by the loss of its three most aggressive leaders.* Thus
the Congressional delegation continued under control of the older

---

* Of the thirty men elected to Congress from Connecticut, twelve were born
before 1734. They died at an average of 77, a median age of 75. Seven were born
in the three years 1736, 1737 and 1738. They died at an average of 59, or a median
of 61. Since the younger men were more aggressive, and much more mercantilist
and nationalist in their interest, surely their relatively early deaths slowed the development of a nationalist party in Connecticut.

leaders, and at the close of the war, an even more fundamentally Calvinist group, largely agrarian in outlook, rose briefly to challenge the dominance of Trumbull, Huntington, Williams, Sherman, and the other Revolutionary spirits.

# The Articles of Confederation

On June 14, 1776, when the Connecticut General Assembly instructed its Congressmen to propose independence, it also asked them to "move and promote, as fast as may be convenient, a regular and permanent Plan of Union and Confederation of the Colonies." This union was to have limited purposes; that is, to provide for "the security and preservation of their just rights and liberties and for mutual defense and security." To this progressive objective was added a limiting proviso, "that the administration of government and the power of forming governments for, and the regulation of the internal concerns and police of each Colony, ought to be left and remain to the respective Colonial Legislatures." Thus the jealous little republic saw Confederation almost as an evil necessity. Were it not for outside threats to liberty, perhaps union would not be desirable at all. After all, the events now unfolding were a contest over the authority of a centralizing government bent on extending its control into the daily lives of peaceable American citizens. Governments were like that, and no new one should be given any potentially despotic powers. The localist sentiment, declared even before independence, was the most durable hallmark of Connecticut's attitude toward union through the whole period of the War and the Confederation. It was complicated, and at times diluted, only by the state's concern over control of its western land claims. Indeed, as a general condition, isolation of the colonies from each other was so strong that the development of inter-colonial cooperation was as surprising as the Revolutionary victory itself.

In Philadelphia, Congress acted on the problems of union and independence on June 11, 1776. On the next day, committees were appointed, one to write a declaration of independence, and another, consisting of one member from each delegation, "to prepare and digest the form of a confederation to be entered into between these colonies." Roger Sherman was Connecticut's member, and thus sat on both of these important committees. The actual drafting of a plan of union was assigned to John Dickinson, who was at this time still opposed to independence. His election must have been due in part to his great reputation as a stylist and in part as a necessary political maneuver to balance the radical dominance on the committee to write the Declaration. In any event, Dickinson did submit a draft, but when Congress voted for independence on July 2, he left that body to return no more.

There were three major points of dispute in regard to the mode of union to be constructed, though on the matter of confederation itself virtual unanimity reigned. The disputed points were: the basis for voting in Congress; the basis for assessing contributions to the general treasury; and the problem of western lands.

Three proposals had been put forth as to how the vote should be taken under the new-proposed government: the populous states called for proportional votes; the small states wanted equal votes, as had been the accepted method thus far; and South Carolina delegates had suggested that votes should be set according to the size of contributions to the Continental treasury. Roger Sherman, a pragmatic compromiser from a state that ranked fifth or sixth out of thirteen, suggested that "the vote should be taken two ways: call the Colonies, and call the individuals, and have a majority of both." Though this ultimately would be instituted in the United States Constitution of 1787 through the mechanics of a two-house congress, Sherman had to wait eleven years to be taken seriously. His essential state orientation, federal rather than national, was explicit in his view that the delegates were "representatives of States, not individuals." He and all the other Connecticut congressmen favored a one-state, one-vote system. With proportional vote, Sherman pointed out that "three Colonies would govern the whole, but would not have the strength to carry these votes into execution." When the issue was finally put to a test in October, 1777, all three Connecticut delegates opted for an equality, thus Congress "decided the great Question in favor of each States having one Vote," wrote William Williams, "tho greatly opposed by a number, and to the great dissatisfaction of Virginia."

On the question of taxation, Connecticut did not make out so well. Contributions might be based on population, wealth, or some combination of both. But wealth was hard to measure: should it be land values? how were wealth and population related? were slaves to be counted as population or property? Roger Sherman insisted that "the number of Inhabitants . . . will be the best that can be devised, . . . The wealth of a people I believe will generally be found to be nearly in proportion to the numbers that can be supported in a State, and wealth principally arises from the labour of men." Williams, too, thought that numbers as the basis of requisitions would be the mode to which there would be the fewest exceptions and the most equitable, "thou' I am certain this is far from perfect."

But was the labor of a slave equal to that of a white man? There was considerable discussion of the matter, with general agreement that it was not. "As to the negroes I should be willing to do as appears equitable," Sherman said. Perhaps those under ten years old should be excluded, he suggested, but something must be done rather than delay confederation. A Virginia member suggested that since a slave worked about half as hard as a freeman, two slaves should equal one free man in tabulating population for reasons of both representation and taxation. The idea was taken up much later in March, 1783. At that time the question of slave computation arose in the context of levying money requisitions on the states, so it was to Connecticut's advantage to count as many of them as possible. At that time the southerners were for counting half of them. Oliver Wolcott moved to make it three-fourths, and Eliphalet Dyer, a slave owner himself, would accept two-thirds. Both, though at first opposing it, finally came to accept the three-fifths ratio. And in 1787, at the Constitutional Convention, Sherman, Oliver Ellsworth, and William Samuel Johnson willingly retained it.

However, all this was to come later. For the time being, Congress adopted as part of the Articles the provision that requisitions would be levied on a formula based on the value of privately-held land and improvements. The final draft containing these provisions was accepted by Congress on November 15, 1777. It must have been a relief to William Williams, who over a year earlier had sighed, "I almost Despair of seeing it accomplished"; and a few days later, "I fear a permanent one will never be settled." But now he could write that "the Plan of Confederation was finished."

Copies of drafts of the Articles began to arrive in Connecticut in the summer of 1776, so that when the final version was sent out by Congress on November 17, 1777, interested Connecticuters had been discussing it for some time. Printed copies were not available until after November 28, and Governor Trumbull received his on December 18. Congress asked for ratification by March 10, 1778, so Trumbull took it up with the Council of Safety. On December 16, the Council ordered three hundred copies to be printed, one to be sent to the selectmen of each town "as soon as possible," and the rest to be given the members of the General Assembly when it met at an adjourned session on January 8.

Within the next three weeks, voters all across Connecticut met in town meeting to discuss the proposed Articles. At least forty-five of these meetings endorsed the draft, and no town is known to have rejected it. There were some objections, however. The principal one, as expected, was the mode of laying requisitions. The Assembly discussed the draft at length, and the House approved it. But the Council did not complete consideration of it in January, so it held over to the next adjourned session that opened on February 12. The Governor noted that the Articles "call first for your attention, and as this business was well neigh completed during your late sessions, I hope it will be speedily finished."

There seems to have been wide agreement in principle on confederation. The Articles, in the opinion of the Assembly, "in general appear to be well adapted to cement and preserve the union of said States, to secure their freedom and independence and promote their general welfare. . . ." All was not quite right, however, and amendments were proposed. Proportionate expenses should be based upon population, not the value of land and buildings, because "trade and manufacturers . . . [are] sources of wealth to a State as well as the produce of lands"; and besides, a just estimate of relative real-estate values would be impossible to determine. A second proposal would qualify Congressional regulation of the army by prohibiting the maintenance of land forces in time of peace or pensioners except for military disability.

The Assembly instructions to the Congressional delegates, however, were ambiguous. That other ratifications might also be qualified by proposed amendments was recognized. But since it was "highly expedient . . . that the Articles of Confederation be finally concluded and ratified as soon as possible," Connecticut empowered her delegates to Congress to ratify "with such amendments, if any be, as by them in conjunction with the Delegates of the other States in Congress shall be thought proper." Presumably, this gave leeway to adopt the draft as it stood, or with amendments of any kind. Connecticut was the second state to authorize ratification; only South Carolina preceeded her. On June 23, the Connecticut Congressional delegates, Sherman and Titus Hosmer, dutifully presented their amendments, but along with all other proposals for alteration at this time, they were rejected. Nevertheless, the Connecticut delegates, with those of all the other states except Delaware, Maryland, and New Jersey, prepared to sign the document. That ceremony was planned for the anniversary of the Declaration of Independence, but a quorum failed to appear, and it was not until July 9 that the delegates from eight states signed.

The Connecticut men who signed the Articles were Sherman, Samuel Huntington, Oliver Wolcott, Andrew Adams, and Titus Hosmer. Wolcott and Huntington had obtained leave on July 7, but apparently stayed until the 9th, and all three joined their signatures to Sherman's and Hosmer's on that day. Actually, a single delegate was permitted to represent Connecticut, and, as the act then stood, any, either or even all of them could be in attendance at any given time.* None of these men was unconscious of history, and even Andrew

---

* An act of May, 1779, which authorized not less than two, nor more than four delegates to represent the state had not yet become effective.

49

Adams, who never had been to Congress before, and who would leave after three months never to return, wanted to be present at the creation.

Four of the signers of the Articles we have met before, but Andrew Adams, one of Connecticut's unsung politicoes, deserves his own sketch, too. Adams, a Yale graduate, practiced law in Litchfield. He developed a distinguished and highly lucrative business, ultimately rising to the chief justiceship of the Superior Court, a position that he held at the time of his death in 1797. He was appointed to the Council of Safety in 1777 and spent a good deal of time at Lebanon, many miles away from hearth and home in Litchfield. He was elected a delegate to Congress for three one-year terms, but served only from August 9, 1778, to January 10, 1779, in which year he was elevated to Connecticut's upper house. Adams finally agreed to go to Congress, but only at a time when he "was fully of Oppinion that the War was drawing to a speedy issue: I looked up on the present campaign," he wrote on the eve of Valley Forge, "as the last and that we had before us every prospect of Success, and our Independ[ence]e as fix'd-." Shortly after arriving in Philadelphia he wrote, "I have as you observe taken a Seat in Congress, and mixd among the great States-Men of America among whose shining Talents you may well imagine my feable Genious is lost in Obscurity." But less than two weeks later he noted curtly to Oliver Wolcott, whom he had replaced, "I can more properly express (orally) than write my Sentiments upon some particular Members."

Connecticut statesmen expected other states to act as quickly as South Carolina had on ratifying the Articles. But they were to be badly disappointed, and no group of American politicians ought to have seen more clearly the cause of delay: western lands. Some states claimed more or less open-ended western limits, and some states had fixed boundaries. Connecticut, with its sea-to-sea charter, was one of the former. Not only was she the claimant to the northern third of Pennsylvania—the Susquehannah lands—but she also held rights to a strip of the continent about seventy miles wide stretching all the way to the Pacific Ocean. Virginia claimed a vast hinterland. In the states having western limits—most notably Pennsylvania, Maryland, and Delaware— large and influential companies of speculators had bought land from Indians. Many of these private claims conflicted with grants made by landed states to their own citizens, and many others lay in territory still claimed by state governments.

Many of the speculators held seats in Congress, mixing private interest with public service, as had Dyer and Deane. They were determined that their investments should be approved by Congress. On the other hand, Congressmen from the landed states wished to make sure that any territory they ceded to the United States should be put to the public benefit rather than private profit. By February, 1779, how-ever, all states had ratified the Articles except Maryland, the principal seat of the speculators. She held out while Virginia revised the terms of her cession of lands, apparently never to Maryland's satisfaction. Finally, however, in February, 1781, under the threat that the Confederation would become operative without her and facing heavy pressure from the British Navy in the Chesapeake Bay, Maryland ratified.

Congress, with President Samuel Huntington in the chair, set noon of March 1 as the time when the Articles would become effective. At that time "The Congress" became "The United States in Congress Assembled," and the states were bound together in a constitutional frame.

## Wyoming and Vermont

THE riches of America in the eighteenth century consisted of land. That is what Europeans fought Indians for during three and a half American centuries. That is what the English English and American English fought the French for in 1754–1763. And that is what Connecticuters and Pennsylvanians were fighting over on the eve of the Revolution.

The Articles of Confederation and Perpetual Union, in its longest and most complicated section, Article IX, established a mechanism for the settlement of just such conflicting land claims, and the case of the Susquehannah settlers is the single instance of the application of this mechanism. The Connecticut delegates consistently battled to avoid a showdown on an issue that seems always to have had an air of fantasy about it. Only Eliphalet Dyer, with his great personal interest in the project, really believed that a favorable judicial outcome was possible. Meanwhile, about three thousand Connecticuters more or less successfully held the soil against attacks by, at one time or another, the Pennsylvania military, mercenaries hired by the Proprietors, British regulars, Indians, floods and fires, and various combinations of these. In 1774, the several settlements around what is now Wilkes-Barre were incorporated as a town—larger than the whole state of Connecticut—and sent deputies to the General Assembly. The town, later made a county, called Westmoreland, raised two companies of militia, was authorized a set of county judicial and civil officers, and in every way acted in orthodox Connecticut fashion. Committees appointed by Congress to settle the controversy got nowhere, and finally, in 1779, Pennsylvania brought an action under the terms of the incompletely-ratified Articles of Confederation.

The Connecticut General Assembly in January, 1780, first instructed its Congressmen to petition for a delay until the war was over "because that sundry Papers of Importance in the Case are in the Hands of Council in England . . . nor is it convenient for the States to divert their attention from the great Objects of the War to attend to private Controversies." A few days later, however, convinced that delay was no longer feasible, the Assembly acquiesed and appointed agents to participate with the Pennsylvanians in the appointment of commissioners to hear the case under the terms of Article IX. At the same session, Dyer, whom the freemen had left out of the delegation, was appointed by the Assembly to the Congressional seat vacated by Andrew Adams. Dyer, then, along with Jesse Root, who was also a Congressman, and William Samuel Johnson, who was not, was instructed to appear before the commissioners and "to do every Thing necessary and proper for the vindication and defence of the Claim and Right of this State to the said Lands in controversy. . . ."

The selection of the Congressional panel took until August, and then some of the members favorable to Connecticut's position did not serve, which Dyer thought a fatal happenstance. The actual trial, which was held at Trenton, New Jersey, did not get under way until the middle of November, 1780. The Connecticut agents then pursued every delaying tactic they could think of, but finally the substance of the matter came before the commissioners. The case brought face to face two of the greatest legal minds of eighteenth-century America, James Wilson and William S. Johnson. Wilson, a Scotsman, had come to America in 1765 at the age of twenty-three with a good classical education. He took up law and land speculation, a pair of handily complementary activities. He was a long-standing member of Congress, and ultimately a justice of the United States Supreme Court under the Constitution of 1787. First and foremost, however, he was a speculator in lands and securities.

William Samuel Johnson was a trail blazer for Anglican acceptance in pre-Revolutionary Connecticut politics. After being graduated from Yale, he studied with his father, one of Connecticut's original Anglican clergymen, but gave up theology for the practice of law. His brilliance and his gracious, temperate style quickly made him a leader of the Connecticut bar. In 1761, he was elected to the lower house of Assembly to represent his home town of Stratford. Then in the Stamp Act upset of '66, because of his conservative respectability and his Fairfield County location, he was chosen by the radical patriots as part of the coalition put together in the successful effort to unseat Governor Fitch and his followers. Johnson was the first Anglican ever to attain a seat on the Council.

52

He represented Connecticut moderates at the Stamp Act Congress in 1765, along with the radical Eliphalet Dyer and the conservative David Rowland, and there he played an influential role. Though the constitutional position adopted by the Congress went beyond what he wished it had in asserting colonial rights to self-government, he supported its proceedings for the sake of unity. The Assembly then sent him to England to defend the Colony's right to vast acreage in eastern Connecticut against the claims of land speculator, John Mason. He spent four years there, developing his affinity for the mother country, the reverse of Eliphalet Dyer whose English sojourn created such distrust of that society. Johnson resumed his seat on the Council in 1772, where he sat until May, 1776, when he failed at reelection, because of Loyalist proclivities. In July, 1779, however, he took the oath of fidelity to the State, and, in an effort at further rehabilitation, the Assembly appointed him to Congress on the resignation of Charles Church Chandler in October. William Williams, who because of his wife's ill health, declined to go to Congress at this time, wrote that the lower house had appointed Johnson, "and the U. House by a small vote concured, some of us think with St. Paul, that He that went not with us in tribulation, may as well stand bye at this Time of Day." Johnson did not attend at that time, but his reform apparently convinced the freemen, and in 1785, 1786, and 1787 he was elected a delegate. Johnson attended for brief terms during those years, accumulating only about twenty months service, but he was the most influential Connecticut Congressman during the downhill phase of that body.

Jesse Root, with Dyer and Johnson, the third agent, was also an accomplished lawyer. A graduate of the College of New Jersey (now Princeton), he, like Johnson, studied for a couple of years for the ministry but gave it up to turn to the bar. Though he grew up in Coventry and reared his own nine children there, he practiced in Hartford. Judging from his convictions on paper money, taxes, and national wealth, his clientele must have been largely mercantile.

Root served on the Council of Safety and was elected to the Connecticut upper house in 1780, resigning nine years later to become Chief Justice of the Superior Court. In 1807, he gave up that post, convinced that public officers should retire while still at the height of their powers. He was then seventy-one years old. In 1789, he began to edit the law reports of Connecticut's higher courts, continuing the series begun by Ephraim Kirby in 1785—the first in America. He served in the state constitutional convention of 1818, where he argued the most extreme conservative position, one which must be allowed a public servant of eighty-two.

Root was first elected to the Congress in 1778 and was continued for five years. He attended for three six-month terms, ending his service in August, 1782. Perhaps by that time he was sick of politics, for he wrote to a friend, "I expect there will be great Governeering among the Candidates, this Spring, and among the many who have Strong pretentions, I hope the good Old Governor will hold possession of the Chair—." Root's conservatism manifested itself not only in his adoration of steady habits, but also in a commitment to strong, efficacious national government. He was a very early nationalist. As early as December, 1780, he wrote his "good Old Governor" that "The union of these thirteen States for their mutual interest and safety constitutes a republic of States or political persons, . . . over which Congress is appointed to preside, and it is as necessary that Congress should exercise the powers of coercion over the particular States for the general purposes of the confederacy as it is . . . that each State should exercise such power over its particular citizens for the weal of the State." And five years later he still hammered away at that theme: "Congress must be vested with competent powers to regulate Trade —to raise a revenue for national purposes to govern this republic of states or we never can perpetuate our union. . . ."

Despite the battery of legal talent sent to New Jersey by Connecticut and the Susquehannah Company, the trial at Trenton was a disaster for both the State and the Company. The decision of the judges was handed down on December 30, 1782, after a long and arduous legal battle. The Connecticut agents put up the best fight they could. Even Johnson, ill much of the time and never fully convinced that he was on the strongest side of the case, was commended for his efforts by the deeply-disappointed Dyer. But Connecticut's claim to jurisdiction over the lands in Pennsylvania was nullified. The significance of the case, however, really goes beyond the substance of it. "This celebrated cause," wrote one editorialist, ". . . presents to the world a new and extraordinary spectacle: Two powerful and populous states, sovereign and independent (except as members of the federal union) contending for a tract of country equal in extent to many, and superior to some European kingdoms. Instead of recurring to arms, the *ultimo ratio* of kings and states, they submit to the arbitration of judges mutually chosen from indifferent states."

Lands to the west were not the only ones that interested Connecticuters in the last quarter of the eighteenth century. Western New Hampshire, or eastern New York—or was it northwestern Massachusetts?—also turned Connecticut heads. After the French and Indian war, large numbers of Yankees with both speculative and homesteading interests migrated to the lands between Lake Champlain and the Connecticut River. The area was claimed by all three bordering colonies, but most Connecticut settlers held their grants from New Hampshire. The area, long known as New Connecticut, was more formally referred to as the New Hampshire Grants. Not only were large numbers of Connecticut citizens economically interested in the area, but the delegates in Congress came to have a political interest there as well. Ultimately, the territory would be admitted as the fourteenth state in 1791, but fifteen years of battle on the floor of Congress preceded that event.

Ethan Allen of Salisbury was a major speculator in lands in the New Hampshire Grants, and the Green Mountain Boys were actually vigilantes organized to combat claimants to the same land under New York grants. Allen, aided and abetted by his Connecticut friends, came to dominate the area after the conquest of Ticonderoga in 1775. Allen then petitioned for statehood, basing his action on a Congressional resolution of 1776 which called upon the colonies "where no government sufficient to the exigencies of their affairs have been established, to adopt such government as shall . . . best conduce to the happiness and safety of their constituents in particular, and in America in general." The description fit Allen's area perfectly. The political interest of Connecticut in supporting such a petition lay in the desire to establish the precedent of dismembering a state—in this case New York or New Hampshire—in order to strengthen its claim to Pennsylvania's Wyoming Valley. In June, 1777, Roger Sherman, who became the principal Green Mountain advocate at Congress, introduced the Vermont petition requesting recognition as an independent state eligible to send Congressional delegates.

The New Yorkers were furious, and James Duane, who had large speculative holdings in the area, raised very hot opposition. Duane was a worthy opponent of the crafty Sherman. John Adams characterized him as a man of "sly, surveying eye, a little squint-eyed . . . very sensible . . . and very artful." Duane was successful in asserting the New York claim, and wrote a friend: "Yesterday the Committee of the whole House finished their proceedings concerning our Revolters and reported them to the House. An unexpected field of debate was opened and some of our neighbors ( R. S. in particular ) discovered an earnestness and solicitude that did not belong to Judges between a State and its discontented members. But it was of little avail to object. . . ." Duane, however, could not have been opposing two more dauntless fellows—Allen and Sherman. The case was kept open by one device or another, and rattled around the closets of Congress keeping the Yorkers on edge.

Finally, in the fall of 1780, after Gates' disastrous humiliation at the hands of Cornwallis at Camden, the Vermonters threatened to make a separate peace with England. Congress had to take the Green Mountain people seriously; and so they did. Acting on a committee report written by Sherman, Congress called on New York and New Hampshire to follow the example of Massachusetts and give up their claims to Vermont. Things looked promising for Allen, but there now developed an unbreakable coalition of southerners who disliked the idea of more northern votes, along with Pennsylvania delegates who feared the precedent of dividing states, and of course New York and New Hampshire. Thus, the matter was not settled until all the other land questions had been resolved, and indeed, until a new government had been established for the United States. Connecticut, then, could not save Vermont or Wyoming for her emigrants, though eventually most of those already settled and on the spot would gain legal title to their lands. But there was a lot of land in America and Connecticut still thought she owned a large piece of it. As we shall see later, she was to bite off a big hunk that Congress grudgingly let her chew.

## Continental Finance

W ARS, as everyone knows, cannot be fought on spirit alone; where there is will there must also be ways and means. Of all the wonders of the Revolutionary era, perhaps the greatest was the monetary miracle of financing a war without an income. In working this fiscal phenomenon, the Connecticut delegates at Congress and the hard-headed deputies in the General Assembly back home were tremendously influential. It should be recalled that Connecticut was thought to be the fifth most populous state after North Carolina and the big three of Virginia, Pennsylvania, and Massachusetts.* Connecticut's well-developed agricultural land and commercial activities generally placed it ahead of North Carolina in estimates of wealth. Thus she found herself more heavily burdened than any other state on a per capita basis, and thus her delegates took a great interest in fiscal affairs.

The colonies throughout the eighteenth century had always resorted to the issuance of fiat money during wartime, and it was only natural that Congress should do the same in 1775. By the end of 1776, twenty-five thousand paper dollars† had been issued, backed only by the good faith of the colonies, each of which, starting in 1779, was supposed to collect a quota of the bills and return them to Congress. By

---

* The census of 1790 revealed that New York had a greater population throughout the 1780's, but that was not known during the earlier period.

† At various times all the colonies had emited money in pounds and shillings, but at differing values, so Congress used the Spanish dollar—pieces of eight—as its medium. Roger Sherman drew up a table of relative values of all other specie to dollars at the request of Congress.

1777, however, the money had begun to depreciate. In April of that year it took two dollars to buy one dollar's value in hard currency, and before official devaluation was effected, one silver dollar would buy 167 paper dollars; indeed, in some back-country villages it fell to five hundred to one before a new government arose to support it.

DEPRECIATION OF OLD CONTINENTAL CURRENCY

(Paper Currency Required to Purchase $1.00 Specie)

|          | 1777  | 1778   | 1779  | 1780  | 1781   |
|----------|-------|--------|-------|-------|--------|
| January  | 1.25  | 4.00   | 8.00  | 42.50 | 100.00 |
| April    | 2.00  | 6.00   | 16.00 | 60.00 | 167.50 |
| July     | 3.00  | 4.00*  | 19.00 | 62.50 | —      |
| October  | 3.00  | 5.00   | 30.00 | 77.50 | —      |

* The temporary increase in value in 1778 reflects the signing of the French treaty that year.

Early in 1777, Congress requested the states to designate its paper as legal tender, to accept it for taxes, and to establish uniform rates of exchange between it and other kinds of money. Governor Trumbull reported to President Hancock that these measures had already been taken, and in May the Assembly also prohibited the circulation in Connecticut of currency from any other state, a measure that local merchants had been promoting for twenty-five years. Virtually all the Connecticut leaders at this time had mercantile backgrounds, and by long experience had learned the benefits of a stable medium. Governor Trumbull, though personally deeply in debt, wrote the Connecticut delegates that the "remedy for the public is the same as for a private person,—that is, to pay his debt when 'tis in his power." Taxation, he declared, "is the plain path for us." Roger Sherman, the leading fiscal conservative in Connecticut, and for several years a major figure in Congressional fiscal policy, made the point over and over in debate upon the floor and in letters home to deputies in the Connecticut Assembly. "Taxing high and often," he insisted, was the best way to defray the expenses of the war. The people, he thought, "in general are convinced of the necessity of it."

Indeed, Connecticut was most responsible in fiscal matters. Though the General Assembly issued paper money with a £457,250 face value between 1775 and 1780, it always levied heavy taxes to sink them. Taxes, indeed, rose to astronomical figures. In some cases, a single levy appeared to amount to 25 per cent of a person's estate, though of course the estate was accounted in specie values, and the tax could be paid in depreciated paper.* Nevertheless, in October, 1777, the Assembly instructed her Congressional delegates to move that all states tax themselves sufficiently to sink their own and some of the Continental emissions, and to put the war on a pay-as-you-go basis. Congress complied in part, and set Connecticut's quota of Continental bills at £600,000. The Assembly thought the proportion unfair, but could hardly object to her own suggestion. Two shillings on the pound was levied to do the job.

Other modes of sinking state and Continental paper were suggested from time to time, but the General Assembly and Connecticut's delegates in Congress continued to see taxation as the only real solution. While waiting for the January, 1780, financial report, the delegates wrote Trumbull that they had detained the regular post rider, Jesse Brown, in order to have some news to send home, "lest his return without any intelligence might fix the impression on the minds of the people that Congress was only amusing them with bare pretences. . . ." They were happy to transmit resolutions that they hoped would "wholly remove those impressions, and as by the co-operation of the people and the blessing of God will give perminent credit to our bills. . . ." As soon as Brown arrived in Hartford with the Congressional quotas, the Assembly laid taxes totalling five shillings on the pound, "although the sum of seventeen hundred thousand dollars is considered as more than the proportion of this State." Governor Trumbull, too, began to balk, protesting that such a contribution would be "exceedingly difficult if not impracticable." But Roger Sherman was the Congressman responsible for setting the quotas, and of course the delegates supported the Continental position, refusing even to support a remonstrance sent to Congress by the General Assembly.

Either the people did not cooperate, or God did not bless the project—or both—for inflation continued to rage. The Connecticut delegates led the way in bringing about an end to emissions. Roger Sherman wrote a committee report for Congress in June, 1779, calling for the cessation of issues of Continental money and for a Congressional request to the states to do the same. Sherman at that time called for the redemption of Continental bills in gold and silver, and later pointed out that a tax of only one shilling on the pound across the whole United States would pay the entire debt in twelve years. He was the hardest of hard money men at Congress, and perhaps a bit of a dreamer, too. Even Spencer and Huntington voted against him at this time.

* Indeed, in the twelve months following the middle of 1780, the local tax collector was supposed to be gathering thirteen different levies totalling eighty-four shillings and five pence on each pound of assessed valuation. In other words, a taxpayer had to pay well over four times the value of his property in a single year's taxes. However, only the five pence had to be specie; all the rest could be paid in the heavily-depreciated paper.

58

By early 1780, however, the inefficacy of all efforts to support paper currency had to be admitted. "The failure of that great resource, the press, gives as was expectable a violent shock," wrote young Oliver Ellsworth to Governor Trumbull, "but it is hoped will prove a salutary one." Congress swallowed hard and, in a report written by Ellsworth himself, called for redemption of the debt at forty for one. But even this failed, and the old money fell to two-hundred to one, ultimately to five-hundred to one, virtually worthless till partially resuscitated by the new government after 1789.

Oliver Ellsworth, a new young delegate, was first elected to Congress in 1777 and was chosen six more times, the last in 1783. He had a lucrative law practice in Hartford, but was prevailed upon to go to Congress and served about sixteen months over a five-year period. His administrative ability was immediately recognized, and he was appointed, at one time or another, to every one of the Congressional executive boards. In 1783, as a result of his work with the pressing financial problems, he was offered the influential, but equally arduous, post of Commissioner of the Treasury, a board of three which was to replace a single Treasurer. But by this time Ellsworth was back in private practice in Hartford, and had no desire to return to the financial tangles of a bankrupt Congress. Though unwilling himself to serve, Ellsworth was beginning to see the need of an energetic central government. Reflecting upon the "calamities of a disunion and anarchy," in 1783, Ellsworth wrote Oliver Wolcott, that "there *must*, Sir, be a revenue somehow established, that can be relied on, and applied for national purposes, as the exigencies arise, independent of the will or views of a single State, or it will be impossible to support national faith or national existence. The powers of Congress must be adequate to the purposes of their constitution. It is possible, there may be abuses and misapplication, still it is better to hazard something, than to hazard all." He would have a chance to implement his views in Philadelphia four years later.

Ellsworth was right about the state of national finances, and after 1783 the war debts became the major concern of the Confederation Congress. All sorts of obligations had to be paid. There were notes due to officers and enlisted men for wages, bonuses and pensions; accounts with commissary quartermaster, hospital, and other officers who had disbursed money during the war; and debts owed to individual suppliers. In addition, there were United States securities on foreign and domestic private loans, and very large accounts with state governments that had paid war expenses for the common cause. The total was in the tens of millions of specie dollars, but Congress had no revenue with which to pay it.

It was thought for a time that the sale of the national domain would provide a source of income, but the land cessions were delayed so long that creditor patience with the Confederation government wore out first; and land sales would have brought but a small sum, anyway. Direct taxation was a political impossibility, and, in any event, was not permitted under the Articles of Confederation. The most viable mechanism—politically, administratively, and fiscally—for obtaining a national revenue was an import duty, or impost as it was called. The impost came riding into Connecticut in tandem with a proposal to pension Continental officers, and terribly upset local politics throughout the crucial Confederation decade.

An impost duty was the darling of fiscal conservatives from a date about mid-point in the war. It was first broached in Congress in a report of September 19, 1778, written by Robert Morris of Pennsylvania, who in the end was to be appointed a sort of financial dictator. He suggested a two per cent ad valorem duty on all imports to be collected by Congress. Little note was taken of the suggestion at that time, largely because it would have meant an augmentation of Congressional authority at a time when even the Articles of Confederation had not been fully ratified. Such a duty was again proposed during the debate culminating in the March 18, 1780, act that ended fiat issues, but it was defeated nine states to two. The impost idea was revived again in August, 1780, when one Connecticut man referred to it as "a Scheme in Embryo."

The next time the question arose it was in the context of granting Congress increased powers, but only the sponsors of the resolution, North Carolina and New Jersey, and New York and Connecticut, then represented by high nationalists Jesse Root and Oliver Wolcott, voted in favor. Root wrote Governor Trumbull at the end of 1780 that he saw no fair and efficacious way to raise money for the Congress but "by duties and imposts in the Continental way." Wolcott at about the same time suggested that "a superintending power destitute of any estate, any funds, any power to establish such, or to controll or regulate the money of a country, is perhaps a novelty in the history of mankind," Congress was discussing, he reported, a resolution asking the states for a grant of authority "to regulate all foreign commerce, to impose such dutys on trade as Congress shall think proper *pro bono publico* ... ." Though not willing to expand Congressional powers generally, the members did request the states to grant a five per cent impost at this time, February 3, 1781.*

Samuel Huntington, as President of Congress, sent the resolve on to the states requesting their prompt compliance, and reminding them of the "Train of Embarrassments, too tedious to need Enumeration . . .

---

* Of course, the impost would not solve all of Congress' financial problems. It was estimated that a five per cent duty would raise only six to seven hundred thousand specie dollars at a time when the annual interest on the United States debt was about two million.

which have already been felt in a Degree and must greatly increase." Ellsworth and Wolcott told the Governor that "Congress have considered it to be indispensibly necessary that they have some established funds on which to depend," thus pointing to a central element in this bill—an independent revenue for the United States Government. And, they continued, "among the ways and means of effecting this none appeared more natural, easey, and equitable than imposts and duties on articles imported into the country. . . ."

The states, however, were not so compliant as Huntington hoped. Congress jogged them in April, and by July, 1782, when Maryland allowed the impost, only Georgia and Rhode Island remained uncommitted. In November, Rhode Island again refused the grant of authority, and in December, Virginia and Maryland rescinded their approval.

In Connecticut, however, affirmative action was quick in coming, despite some strong opposition in the Assembly. On February 21, 1781, the Governor convened a speeial session, a major concern of which was the impost. The suspicious provincials protested the undermining of republican principles that they saw in this accretion of power in the central government. James Wadsworth, until recently the state's highest militia officer, said that the impost "would lay the foundation for the ruin of the Liberties of the U. States." But the pro-impost deputies managed a majority, and Connecticut became the first state to grant the Congressional request.

The nationalists, however, did not have things all their way, and had to make two qualifying compromises. One gave Connecticut authority to suspend or remove collectors in case of misconduct; the other provided that the act would continue in force for only three years after the war. President Huntington pointed out to Governor Trumbull that the three-year limitation "doth not comport with the resolution of Congress or answer the design of it." Oliver Wolcott was "much surprised that Connecticut had adopted that measure in so partial a manner, not only as I am fully convinced that it is the only mode by which a Tax of this kind can be equitably laid. But as our States consume much more than they Import they have a particular interest in adopting the measure. . . ."

By April, 1783, the states had not fully complied, and Congress had to urge them on again. Connecticut had altered its authorization by removing the three-year limit, but still insisted on other restrictions. Sherman, indeed, was becoming impatient. He wrote in January, 1784, that the only practical way to raise a revenue was through an impost that "takes it at the fountain head and the consumer pays it insensibly and without murmuring." Sherman wished to combine sound fiscal policy with his precious provincial autonomy, however. He told William Williams that "it appears to me that a general impost will be the best way for raising a revenue for the interest of the national debt, though I never wish to have the power in Congress to raise money extended beyond what may be necessary for the present debt, . . . never to raise any for current expenses." He finally got so angry that he suggested that all the states which had allowed the impost should go ahead and implement it and embargo those that had not.

In May, 1784, Connecticut passed the act in terms requested by Congress, but since the authorization was conditional on unanimity among the states, the Assembly wrote its own act levying a five per cent impost on enumerated goods coming into Connecticut by land or sea.

In March, 1786, Georgia approved the request, and so did New York. But the latter's approval was so set about by qualifications—principally that she collect and keep the duties herself—that it really amounted to a rejection. Later pleas from Congress only brought stronger insistence from New York that she do it entirely her way, and Stephen Mix Mitchill remarked that that state had "step'd as t'were out of their way to give Congress a Slap in the face." Though Congress appointed a committee to write an implementing ordinance, nothing ever came of it, and, like the funding of the national debt, a continental impost had to wait till a new government was organized. But the phantom money had carried America to a successful conclusion of the war—and beyond. Who can gainsay as fiscal fantasy policies so fruitful?

## The Commutation Revolt

CONNECTICUT's repeated rejection of a Continental impost does not comport with her well-deserved reputation as the soundest of the fiscally-responsible states. That Congressional request, however, did not come along alone, but arrived instead with some rather bad company. The malodorous consort was life-time pensions for the Continental officers—the basis for an American "aristocracy," as many thought, and an anathema to Connecticut's republican yeomen.

There was nothing new about pensions and pensioners. The British Crown had for centuries granted its retired civil and military officers various annual stipends, customarily amounting to half pay. David Wooster, the darling of Connecticut's military establishment, after all, had been a half-pay pensioner of the Crown, and the American colonies abounded with English gentlemen farmers living on the king's largess. But, as the Simsbury town meeting pointed out, "one great Cause of our late war is well known to be ye exorbitant and unreasonable Pensions granted to particular persons; so it must be supposed for the Honble Continental Congress to grant Such Pensions will be Dangerous alarming & unconstitutional."

George Washington himself started the whole thing in 1778 when he told Congress that without a lifetime half-pay pension "your Officers will moulder to nothing, or be composed of low and illiterate men void of the capacity for this or any other business." Most Congressmen were willing to grant the General whatever he wanted, but some—notably New Englanders—reflected the Simsbury view. As a compromise, Congress voted half pay for seven post-war years to those Continental officers who would serve till the end of the conflict. Noncommissioned officers and men were to receive a bonus of eighty dollars upon discharge. Connecticut's delegates—Huntington, Sherman, and Wolcott—knew full well the temper of their constituents. The Assembly only three months earlier, February, 1778, in approving the Articles of Confederation, had stipulated "that no land army shall be kept up by the United States in time of peace, nor any officers or pensioners be kept in pay by them who are not in actual service," except for those wounded in action.

The issue had been debated heatedly for seven weeks before the compromise was agreed to, and the Connecticut delegates wrote Governor Trumbull that it was "the most painful and disagreeable question that hath ever been agitated in Congress." They had argued, they reported, against "the dangerous tendency of such a measure as being totally inconsistent with free States, repugnant to principles upon which this great controversy was begun and by which it must and ought to be defended." The resolution, they concluded, "is not the best measure the nature and circumstances of the case would admit, [but] it is certainly the best that could be obtained." Wolcott, however, a stronger nationalist than either of his colleagues, voted for the original bill, with James Lovell of Massachusetts, the only New England defections.

The war was not to be over for some time, of course, so the actual payment of the pensions was still a long way off. In the meantime, in October, 1780, Congress had gone back to the lifetime provision of the original proposal. Samuel Huntington was surprised and distressed. "I have ever been opposed to pensions for life as a reward for [army officers'] services, as inconsistent with the genious and spirit of our constitution," he wrote Trumbull. "I presume this resolution will give general satisfaction to the officers, and those who oppose it will incur their disesteem, and perhaps censure; but I am much more concerned on account of its consequences among the people. What effects it will have with them time will best discover; hope it may be better than my fears."

Time discovered, however, that the pension bill would have an effect among the people far worse than Huntington's fears. The issue was to deepen divisions in Connecticut between the nationalists and the provincials, the old agrarian Calvinists and the progressive, more worldly elements. Indeed, it was shortly to bring about the temporary eclipse of the old Revolutionary leadership, now representing a middle position, for the last word had not been heard in either Congress or Connecticut.

In October, 1781, Cornwallis surrendered his main body of troops to Washington, and though neither side knew it at the time, this was to be the last significant engagement of the war. Then, in March, 1782, Lord North's war policy was repudiated by Commons and he was replaced by the conciliatory Rockingham. As news of these events reached Congress it became clear that the war would soon be over. The pensions problem would then become real, and in August a wrangle was precipitated by the Connecticut delegates.

In response to a petition from the Connecticut officers of the Continental line, Jesse Root brought in a resolution that would transfer to the states the half-pay obligation—"Congress having no funds provided for discharging the same." Dyer pointed out that states could then do whatever conformed to the habits of their people. In Connecticut "they wanted to be discharged. They would settle with their own officers and satisfy them and then wanted to have done with it." Root added that "the genius of [Connecticut] people would not brook the paying of annual pensions, that they could not bear to see men strutting about their streets in the port of masters who had a right to demand of the people a part of their annual labor and toil to support them in idleness. That they chose rather to pay their officers at once after the war and then see them descend into the class of citizens." There was no compromise at this time, though Root and Dyer tried again. The debate continued over into the new year and finally came to a head in the early spring of 1783. Oliver Wolcott and Eliphalet Dyer were then representing Connecticut in Congress, and Dyer's seat became the hottest place in America.

A compromise was reached that would have the lifetime half-pay pensions commuted to a lump sum payment of five years' salary. It became known as "the commutation bill," and wracked first Dyer and then his suspicious home state. The vote on the bill was seven states for, three against, with Connecticut split, Dyer conforming to Connecticut Assembly instructions and Wolcott spurning them. The bill would require nine affirmative states to pass; Delaware was absent, but would vote aye. Dyer was under tremendous pressure from his colleagues, and he faced, in addition, a rising discontent among Continental officers then contemplating mutiny at Newburgh, New York. He told General Alexander McDougall, a member from New York, that he would vote for the bill and resolve the issue as soon as the Delaware delegates arrived. When they did, Dyer moved the question, but undergoing the worst tortures of divided loyalties, reversed himself and stayed loyal to his Connecticut constituents. His behavior astonished some members of Congress, and McDougall promised to "tell him in plain terms, in what light the Army and all honest Men must consider his Conduct, if he persists in it."

The question was put again several days later and James Madison tells us: "On the question of paying the Army we had eight States, it required nine. It turned on the vote of Connecticut. These representatives were Dyer, a man of gentlemanly manners, who had seen the world (he had been to England) but not of very sound principle. Wolcott, an honest man. Wolcott determined he would brave the storm that awaited him at home. Dyer hung back. He was of course very much pressed. At length, he consented, on condition that it should be referred to a committee, and that he should be allowed to write a preamble. In this he was indulged." The measure was voted on again with Dyer's preamble, which was the butt of considerable caustic comment, while Dyer, Madison says, "was kept for an hour as pale as a sheet." "How it will be received I know not," Dyer wrote home, "but hope for the best."

Meanwhile, word arrived that the American Commissioners, Franklin, Adams, and Jay, had concluded preliminary articles of peace with England on November 30, 1782. These became effective on January 20 when the British signed agreements with France and Spain. A cease fire was proclaimed for February 4. The provisional treaty arrived from the Commissioners in France on March 13 and was ratified by Congress on April 11. The final draft would be ratified on January 14, 1784, when James Wadsworth and Roger Sherman arrived at Congress to make up a quorum.

The war against Britain was over. But in Connecticut, a major political battle had just begun. Pensions neither paid nor commuted were Connecticut's style, as her Congressional delegates had pointed out time and time again. But the freemen of Connecticut didn't have to be reminded. All across the state, through the Congressional debate of 1782 and 1783, town after town passed resolutions protesting the commutation. They objected that the Continental officers were getting pensions while the men were not, and that the militia, men and officers, were left out altogether. They objected that the officers had been well paid during the war; that aristocracy would be engendered through the grants; that heavy financial burdens would be placed upon the people—and all this without their consent. And they objected that the act was unconstitutional because Congress had gone beyond the explicit intent of the Articles of Confederation.

The war, after all, had been kind of a Christian crusade, and now in the moment of triumph God was to be thwarted. The Norwich town meeting, as an example, praised God for bringing the war to a successful close and enabling Americans "by Divine Aid to Exercise all the Civil priviledges & immunities granted to a free people by indulgent Heaven," and noted that the granting of the people's tax monies by Congress "is a Contradiction in Terms" because it causes "one freeman to Compell another to act freely or Generously; and at once destroys the Idea of Liberty & Freedom out of the world." Norfolk told its deputies to remonstrate against "Paying the commutation Granted . . . as unconstitutional and an Event that is Very Alarming to free Citizens. . . ." Winchester resolved "that we are of the Opinion that the Commutation is unconstitutional & altogether unjust & unreasonable." Town after town sent similar outraged instructions to Hartford.

Of course, commuted pensions would be paid out of revenue to be raised by the aborted five per cent impost. This taught again the lesson of 1765 that a remote government must never be given an independent income or the power to legislate for the provinces. It was just the issue that the agrarian provincials needed to unseat the increasingly unpopular commercial and nationalist clique that had been determining policy for the state since 1774. Oliver Wolcott wrote his son that the anti-establishment forces had planned to exclude seven of the twelve incumbent councilors. "My fate," he wrote, "in case they shall suceed in their Design, I believe I shall acquiese in without a Murmer. . . . To one not acquainted with History, it would appear incredible that those Men, who have acted a more important Part than any other in this State, in bringing the political Vessel safe into Port, . . . should feel the keenest Resentment of that People who were to participate [in] all the Benefit resulting from their Toil and Peril."

The elections did indeed bring a political upset, and altered Connecticut's representation in Congress fundamentally. Dyer, Root, Wolcott, and others all came under the gun. Not only were their Congressional seats on the firing line, but so were their places on the Council. Dyer, the most double dealing of them, actually lost the Councilorship that he had held for over twenty years. Many of the second-level, up-and-coming commercial-national people were also replaced in line of succession by opponents of commutation and the impost. Indeed, so surprising had been the strength of the anti-nationalists, and so unusual was it in Connecticut to deny reelection to top state officers, that Samuel Huntington, Richard Law, Oliver Ellsworth, and Oliver Wolcott all resigned in October, rather than wait until the first Monday in November when their statutory limit would run out, so that the Assembly could appoint men more of its own new stamp. Four were appointed: two old and two new. All of these were thought to be anti-commutation men, except Roger Sherman.

William Williams and William Hillhouse did not attend Congress at this time, but Sherman and arch provincial James Wadsworth, spokesman for all the Connecticut militia, did. Sherman was immediately placed upon a committee to survey the commutation issue. Sadly he wrote to Trumbull: "The question is not whether Congress are vested by the Confederation with a power to grant half pay for life. This need not be enquired into. It is whether by the 12th article* of the Confederation they can do otherwise than to acknowledge that a debt was created by the resolution of 21st October 1780 which resolution was agreed to by persons having plenipotentiary powers from their respective States, to do whatever appeared to them necessary and expedient for opposing the enemy effectually." So finally the pensions were granted. By 1786, Continental soldiers had been paid on the average two hundred to three hundred dollars, and officers received sums ranging from about fifteen hundred to ten thousand dollars, depending on rank.

The old-timers paid a price for their violation of the Connecticut spirit in the matter. Those who had not been rejected at the polls were cut out of Congress by other means. The Assembly, in 1784, prohibited simultaneous appointment to Congress and to the newly-created Superior Court. Sherman preferred his judicial appointment and very reluctantly resigned his Congressional seat in May, 1785. Also hit by this provision were Samuel Huntington, Richard Law, William Pitkin, and Oliver Ellsworth. Thus, most of the old timers were no longer eligible to serve in Congress, and after 1784 Connecticut was represented by younger, less well-established men—though the Tory, William Samuel Johnson, working away at his own rehabilitation, was there to guide and lead them.

# The Western Reserve

ONE of the reasons impelling Connecticut's old revolutionaries toward a Congress way back in 1774 was concern over their western land claim. The matter had been more or less before them for the decade of war that followed, and so far it had been a loosing battle. But the defeat of the Susquehannah claims in 1782 meant by no means that all was lost. In the first place, though Connecticut lost jurisdiction over the territory, the settlers there were still to have their day in court. They had an ardent advocate in Congress, too, in the gnarled shape of

* Article XII holds Congress responsible for all debts contracted before the ratification of the Articles of Confederation.

rustic Roger Sherman, perhaps the most politically adept member of the body of adept politicians. "He is as cunning as the Devil," said a Connecticut political enemy, "and if you attack him, you ought to know him well; he is not easily managed, but if he suspects you are trying to take him in, you may as well catch an Eeel by the tail."

The Connecticut settlers in the Wyoming Valley, of which by now there were thousands, could be used as a hostage to Pennsylvania's cooperation in Sherman's plans. Connecticut still regarded the seventy mile wide strip west of Pennsylvania at least to the Mississippi, if no longer to the Pacific, as hers. To sustain this claim was not going to be easy, however, and after the Trenton decision it is doubtful that many knowledgeable Connecticuters really thought they could. It was a vital matter, nevertheless, to hold on to enough land to compensate Connecticut militiamen and the families whose property had been ravaged during the British raids.

The western lands question had blocked Maryland's ratification of the Articles of Confederation because that state insisted that the landed states give up their claims to the central government of the United States. But since Virginia's delegation thought that this might confirm title of Maryland's many large speculators to lands then claimed by state governments and some of Virginia's citizens, Virginia refused to go along. Congress, in a pair of resolutions of September 6 and October 10, 1780, had requested cessions, and had provided that the territory would be "laid out in separate and distinct States. . . ." In October, the Connecticut General Assembly was willing to meet Maryland's demands half way. Rights to soil would be surrendered —i.e., legal authority to survey, sell, and transfer title—but the State was to retain jurisdiction. Congress could raise a revenue in the great western territory, but Connecticut would govern it. These reservations fell far short of Congress' request, and as James Madison wrote, "clog the cession with . . . conditions which greatly depreciate it, and are the more extraordinary as their title to the land is so controvertable a one." Congress was not amenable to the Connecticut cession and in November, 1781, its Committee of Ways and Means urged her and other reluctant states to give up "all Claims and pretentions . . . without any Conditions or Restrictions whatever."

On the eve of the Trenton meeting Dyer had become desperate. He wrote Governor Trumbull suggesting that the qualifications be taken off the cession. "I am sure it would give great satisfaction to Congress," he wrote, "and imagine it might operate kindly and beneficially in our cause." But Congress held the matter in abeyance till after the Trenton decision of December 30, 1782. Then it was the Assembly's turn to act.

At a special session convened just a few days after word of Trenton reached Connecticut, the Assembly ordered the Connecticut Congressmen "not to proceed any further towards carrying into Execution" the October, 1780, resolution of cession. This was supported by a declaration insisting that Connecticut "has the undoubted and exclusive Right of Jurisdiction and Preemption to all the Lands lying West" of Pennsylvania and east of the Mississippi, "which Claim and Title to make known for the information of all to the end that they may conform themselves thereto." Time was needed to work out a new cession that would leave the State with land enough to compensate her soldiers and plundered citizens.

In October, 1783, Virginia made a grant that was agreeable to Congress. The pressure on Connecticut was becoming intense, but it was not until January, 1784, that a new cession was authorized by the Assembly. This act ceded to the United States all western land claimed by Connecticut except for a section extending 120 miles west from the Pennsylvania line and north-south about seventy miles. The area retained was to be used to "satisfy the Officers and Privates in the Connecticut Line of the Continental Army," and "said Tract of Land so reserved hereafter to be formed into a Government either by itself or with such other Territory thereto annexed as shall be Judged most expedient and beneficial under a free Constitution similar to other of the United States." This act was laid before Congress on May 25 by Roger Sherman, back for his last term under the Articles, and Major General James Wadsworth, doughty agrarian taking his only turn in that body.

Congress was now sitting at Annapolis, and a more inappropriate place to receive these two old provincial rustics cannot be imagined. The delegates from the middle and southern states were delighted with the spot. "The polite Attention of the Gentlemen of the Town," wrote a New Jersey delegate, "Engages all our leisure hours in Visits and Amusements. The Players Exhibit twice a week and there is a Brilliant Assembly or Ball once a fortnight. . . ." At one of these, reported another member, "about two hundred attended and partook of the Feast, after which 13 toasts were drunk under a discharge of 13 cannon." But New Englanders were made of different stuff. One of them wrote home that "the Object of the Inhabitants here is altogether pleasure; . . . Balls, Plays, dining and Tea parties engross the Time of the Ladies, Hunting, Fishing, gaming, Horseracing, etc. that of the Gentlemen." Another New Englander, trying to live on four dollars a day, was disgusted with the "plays, Balls, Concerts, routs, hops, Fandangoes and fox hunting" he found there.

To James Wadsworth, a man "with an antique strictness of morals," the experience was almost traumatic. Though a Yale graduate, he was among the most provincial of the provincials. He came from a line of public servants in Durham, where he was born in 1730, and he continued the hometown family tradition. For about fifty years he was town clerk and served over half a hundred sessions in the Assembly. He became speaker of the lower house and then a member of the Council and was first Comptroller of the State. On David Wooster's death in 1777, Wadsworth became Major General of all Connecticut militia. But he was agrarian, provincial, and outspoken, and with the rise of the nationalists in 1786–1787 he was denied further political office. He opposed the Constitution of 1787 and led the fight against its ratification in Connecticut. When, despite his efforts, Connecticut came under the United States Constitution, Wadsworth refused any further public office, holding that he would not violate his oath to the State. He was elected to the old Congress four times, 1783–1786, but his one five-month experience at Annapolis in the winter and spring of 1784 was as much as he could take.

When Wadsworth and Sherman put before Congress the Connecticut cession with its huge reserved territory, there was considerable chagrin mixed with incredulous mirth among the members. Pennsylvania's Edward Hand wrote his governor that "I am persuaded it will amuse you," and Hugh Williamson of North Carolina noted that "Connecticut having failed in her attempts to cut one degree out of the State of Pennsylvania, has just entered her claim to the Same degree Westward of Pennsylvania. . . ." The act, he added, was "curious." Congress was not agreeable, and once again, in October, 1784, the General Assembly empowered its delegates to cede the land. No Connecticut members were present at Congress from June 4 to December 2, but William Samuel Johnson was appointed at the October session, and Joseph Platt Cook would shortly be on his way. On February 15, Johnson requested Congress to accept the cession, and he was assigned to a committee to work the matter out. But Congress was adamant. Johnson and Cook wouldn't budge, either, so the matter stood stalemated.

But in mid-April, 1785, Massachusetts ceded her even more dubious claims, and since other state claims were south of the Ohio, only Connecticut stood in the way of Congressional efforts to organize the Northwest Territory. Now Congress ignored the Connecticut claim and passed the Land Ordinance anyway. The Assembly doggedly tried to rewrite its cession in acceptable terms. In October, 1785, it voted an act which quaintly referred to the area as "unlocated Lands in the western part of the State," ceding the territory west of a line drawn 120 miles west of Pennsylvania omitting any mention of jurisdiction. A second paragraph instructed the delegates "to hasten a determination in Congress as soon as possible, whether they will accept the proposed Cession of this State of Western Lands or not. . . ." Johnson did his best, but still to no avail. He laid the whole matter out for his governor in a long letter of February 24. The offer, he said, "was strenuously objected to." Congress maintained that it had already received the territory in a cession from Virginia, and had just concluded a treaty with the Indians confirming the United States' title. Besides, Connecticut needed no land to compensate her troops for wartime service because Congress had already arranged that. "To these," Johnson concluded, "are added the original deficiencies of our Title, and the decision at Trenton against it. The Answers we shall give to these Objections we need not state. . . ."

Johnson now dominated the Connecticut delegation. His colleagues through this most ticklish period were men of short experience, and no great legal talent. Two months later no progress was to be reported, but Johnson assured his old friend Sherman that "if Connecticut proceeds in the affair with firmness and prudence, she may yet retain the Boundary she has proposed." But, he added, "something must be determined up on soon, for the reserved Territory will be included in the Sale proposed by Congress." But when nothing had happened by May, the Assembly again rephrased its cession. This time it granted "all the Right Title Interest Jurisdiction and Claim" of the territory, but it still insisted on its western reserve.

All along, there had been an ace up Connecticut's sleeve. Some delegates might have been reluctant to pull it out, but things were getting desperate, and Johnson in Congress and Sherman back in New Haven apparently decided that now was the time to play it. Congress was sitting in New York these days—seven hours by water from New Haven—and matters could easily be coordinated. The ace, of course, was the old Susquehannah settlers still squabbling with their Pennsylvania proprietors. They had been promised a day in court—that is before Congressional commissioners—but the Pennsylvania delegates were attempting to undo Congress' instructions on that matter. They were unsuccessful, but when the time of the hearing arrived, the settlers were under siege from Pennsylvanian claimants, and did not show up. Meanwhile, however, the settlers had forcibly repossessed their estates. Sherman, working through a Pennsylvania connection, Pelatiah Webster, formerly of Lebanon, Connecticut, was trying to arrange a compromise in his best backstage style. The idea was to draw the Pennsylvania delegation into support of Connecticut's reserve in exchange for giving up support of the Susquehannah settlers. The General Assembly in October, 1784, had promised to "countenance and Patronize" the settlers, instructed the Congressmen to "give them all necessary Assistance in the Premises," and requested Governor Griswold to address the State of Pennsylvania "remonstrating against the Barbarities and Cruelties" exercised against them. Sherman, in effect, seems to have been offering to call Connecticut off that line of conduct in exchange for Pennsylvania's support on the reserve issue.

All this became evident when Connecticut and Pennsylvania began to vote together without other support in the spring of 1786 when

Johnson was pushing the matter very hard. James Wilson, a very large speculator himself, had been hired at a whopping three hundred pound fee by the State of Pennsylvania to carry its case against Connecticut's settlers. Stephen Mix Mitchell, now all alone and in his first term at Congress, wrote Johnson, "Will you suffer me to besiege Mr. Willson, on the score of our Western Cession, as soon as I can feel out his hobby horse? You know we are twa bonny Scotch Lads," he said referring to his marital connection, "and very national . . . would it be amiss to obtain his Influence in our favor, even by a little verbal abuse of Wyoming?" The Pennsylvania delegates were told by Johnson or Mitchell that Connecticut might "discountenance the further pretensions of the Delaware and Susquehannah Companies to lands in Penns'a and tend to detach the Real settlers of Wyoming from the more disorderly Parizans of these Companies." This was not impossible because the Wyoming settlers were now split into squabbling radical and conservative factions. Johnson also told the Pennsylvanians that the Susquehannah Company speculators could be persuaded to look further west and that the Assembly would discountenance the settlers in "all farther persuit of Claims in Pennsylvania. . . ." Finally, on May 26, 1786, Johnson, seconded by Mitchell, offered the cession. This time Congress accepted.

A Pennsylvania delegate tried to clear out the underbrush for a Connecticut friend, Jeremiah Wadsworth. "It is understood," he wrote, "that the State of Connecticut will on her part give no further Countenance to the Claims of the State or of her Companies within Penn[sa.] but on the Contrary use Means to induce these Companies to relinquish their pretensions to such Claims. That Penn[sa.] will take the Actual Settlers on the late disputed Territory under protection as Citizens and treat them with Generosity as well as Justice as to their private Rights. That the implied Right of Connecticut to the 120 Miles not ceded will not be questioned by Pennsa. and that Connecticut may find Means from that Source to quiet her Companies with respect to Western Lands. . . . But these things being understood rather than expressed, may be differently conceived of by different Minds, and therefore I cannot pretend to say what Interpretations may hereafter be given on this Subject. In Compromises of this kind it is [fo]und dangerous to go too minutely into Explanations." Johnson, wrote a Connecticut friend, "has accomplished the Connecticut cession against all the Arts, policy and finesse of the ablest politicians in Congress." Word of Congressional acceptance was rushed to Hartford where the Assembly was sitting, and the delegates were authorized to execute the deed.

So Connecticut kept its Western Reserve. Surely it was a major political triumph, for no one pretended that justice should allow one state out of thirteen to snatch a piece of the public domain. It was, one

Virginian said, "nothing but a State juggle contrived by old Roger Sherman to get a side wind confirmation to a thing they had no right to. Some of the States, particularly Pennsylvany, voted for them on the same principle that the powers of Europe give money to the Algerines."

# *Finis*

By the time of Connecticut's "Thermadorian of 1783–84," when the provincial farmers briefly dominated politics, other states too were losing interest in the national union. Day after day—even weeks and months—Congress was paralyzed for lack of a quorum. Between November 4, 1784, and March 1, 1785, there was a quorum on but three days. Connecticut must take her share of the blame for the high rate of absenteeism after the conclusion of the war.

Connecticut delegates had been scrupulous attenders all through the years of struggle, but by 1782 they began to weary. Jesse Root arrived in mid-May, 1782, expecting to stay all summer, which he reminded a friend was "disagreeably Sweating to both body and purse." But he was shortly sent on a mission to the northern states to urge the assemblies to "keep up a constant representation." When he left, not only were New Hampshire, New Jersey, Delaware, and North Carolina unrepresented, but Connecticut as well. This five-day void was the first time since the opening of Congress in September, 1774, that there was not at least one Connecticut delegate on the floor, and usually there were two, often three. But it was not to be the last. Eliphalet Dyer, Benjamin Huntington, and Roger Sherman went to Philadelphia for the second half of 1782, but left in early December. Dyer, who had to go to the Trenton Court, wrote that he was "very sorry our delegates delay so long their coming, as the State must be unrepresented, perhaps for near a month, in a critical season and when they are much wanted. . . . We are unhappy in not keeping up a representation of the New England States, which has been the occasion often of many things passing in Congress very disagreeable to them and contrary to the genius of the people there." The Olivers Ellsworth and Wolcott arrived, however, and cut the void to nine days. The following year fared better with important questions of peace before the Congress, but when the Huntingtons, Benjamin and Samuel, came to the end of their terms on the first Monday of November they left the State unrepresented until the new appointees arrived on January 13. Twenty-three delegates, including Roger Sherman and James Wadsworth, were present to ratify the peace treaty with Great Britain, but then delegates began to disappear again.

But 1784 marks the nadir of Connecticut interest in national affairs. From June 4 to December 2, and from Christmas Eve to January 13, 1785, no Yankee member showed himself at Congress. But, of course, neither did the delegates of many other states. In spite of such pressing matters as Indian affairs, western lands, Continental finances, and the still unhappy Susquehannah settlers, Congress adjourned and left matters in the hands of a Committee of States. The Committee, James Madison wrote to Thomas Jefferson, "consists of Mr. Blanchard, Dana, Ellery, Sherman, DeWitt, Dick, Hand, Chase, Hardy, Spaight and Reed . . . the members may also relieve each other at pleasure . . . the powers of the committee are confin'd so that no injury can be effected. Sherman and Dana will necessarily govern it." But Sherman had long since made up his mind to leave as soon as Congress adjourned, and he, along with virtually all other Congressmen, departed. The Committee of States had a quorum on only one day, June 4. For Connecticut's leading Congressman, it was a final farewell to government under the Articles. He would return to national service to help frame a stronger government, and then to serve in turn in its Congress.

All was not over, however, for the national association. Attendance was indeed irregular through the years 1785–1788, but important matters came before the Connecticut delegation, William S. Johnson, Stephen Mix Mitchell, and Joseph Platt Cooke. The western land cessions were completed and the national domain organized under the Northwest Land Acts of 1785 and 1787; a small army was established; Indian relations were rationalized; and executive committees appointed and organized.

Nevertheless, the nationalism that had begun to appear among the commercial elements of Connecticut's political structure as early as the late seventies continued to find expression from influential figures, even through the era of agrarian-provincial dominance of the mid-eighties. As a matter of fact, 1786 marks a year of fragile balance between the two factions. When Congress endorsed the Annapolis call for a new convention to strengthen the Articles, much of Connecticut's leadership was reluctant to accede. The nationalists were fearful that less central authority, rather than more, might result, and of course the provincials feared the reverse. But in the end a delegation was sent. Neither high nationalists nor stalwart provincials, Roger Sherman, William S. Johnson, and Oliver Ellsworth, seasoned congressmen all, went off to write finis to the "Old Congress."

The Congressional experience was an important one for Connecticut politicians. With a single exception—James Wadsworth—those men who had gone to Congress were more nationally-oriented than those who had not. And generally speaking, the younger the delegates were when they entered Congressional service, the more nationalist they became. Thus, Dyer and Williams, old men, were reluctant supporters of the Constitution of 1787, while Jeremiah Wadsworth and Pierpont Edwards, for instance, were ardent.

But not only the leadership learned what a central government could do; so did the tax-paying republican yeomen of Connecticut's inland towns and villages. The agitation over commutation deeply colored Connecticut attitudes toward union and centralization of power. It is significant that of seventeen men elected to Congress after the agrarian take-over of October, 1783, ten never attended at all, and five of the seven who did were old-timers. The two new members were youthful Jeremiah Wadsworth and Pierpont Edwards, and they attended only in 1788, after the new constitution had been ratified in Connecticut.

It is difficult to determine whether nationally-oriented men chose to attend Congress from 1774 to 1788, while the provincially-minded chose to stay at home, or if Connecticuters became nationalist through their Congressional experience. Roger Sherman and his near contemporary Samuel Huntington are examples of the latter possibility; Jonathan Trumbull, Titus Hosmer, Jesse Root, and Silas Deane, all exact contemporaries, are examples of the former. Virtually the entire leadership during the second half of the eighteenth century were either merchants or lawyers, or both in the same person. The less nationalist, however, in addition to being older also, like Williams, S. Huntington and Sherman, conducted modest retail business; while the high nationalists were broader in their mercantile scope, usually importers of consequence like Trumbull and Deane, or lawyers like Root who served them. The high nationalist thrust was considerably weakened by the deaths of Hosmer and Trumbull, and the exile of Deane. In addition, other young nationalists such as John Trumbull and Jeremiah Wadsworth were abroad during the crucial years of 1783 and 1784. The provincials, almost universally, had no Congressional service, and were much more likely to have been militia rather than Continental officers.

There are discernable patterns, then, and since the provincial pattern clearly represents the overwhelming number of Connecticut freemen, why did the state constitutional convention vote 128 to 40 for a stronger central government? The principal factor is undoubtedly the tradition of deference that dominated Connecticut politics until the 1790's. Since the activist leadership element was predominantly nationalist, it was able to carry the day. A second important factor no doubt was the natural conservatism of the agrarian population that not only would lead them to oppose change in general, but would also disincline them to organize to maintain it. They lacked lines of communication, and no Connecticut newspaper would publish their compositions. Third, a most important factor, was Shays' Rebellion in western Massachusetts right over the Connecticut line. This frightened not only the men of mercantile interest, but many moderates whose property was in real estate, and the "Rebellion" went a long way toward allaying the fears of centralization brought on by commutation. And, if reason really sways men's minds, the economic advantages to Connecticut consumers, as well as to her merchants, that would result from a national free-trade area were clearly great. Finally, Sherman and Ellsworth apparently convinced the generally more provincially-oriented holders of state bonds that their credits would be paid to them by the new central government. Thus, the Old Congress government, for which no one in Connecticut had any deep attachment, was easily rung out and the new rung in despite the vastness of the agrarian-provincial majority among the state's freemen.

But what a school yard the "Old Congress" had been! All but one of the Connecticut congressmen elected in 1788 were former delegates, and indeed the old men of experience dominated the delegation until the mid-1790's. There they practiced the lessons they had learned about the benefits of a national impost, interstate courts, executive offices, and departments for foreign affairs, treasury, and post office.

Though their complaints about money shortages and high taxation were loud, 1783–1787 were not crisis years for most Connecticut farmers. Probably they would just as well have left the national government as it was, or even done without one altogether. But lawyers and merchants cared, and in a state guided by a small group of such men, and dominated by a tradition of deference to the wealth, education, and family that they represented, it was possible for the minority to rule. And without that leadership there would have been no Revolution, no Continental Congress, no United States Constitution—and, who knows, by now maybe no Connecticut.

76

This short pamphlet is intended for the general reader, and represents a summary and interpretation of prior scholarship, not a report of new findings. Fundamental to any study of the Continental Congress are Edmund Cody Burnett's two major works, *The Continental Congress* (New York, 1941) and *Letters of Members of the Continental Congress* (Washington, 1921–38). Perhaps as many as two-thirds of the quotations found here are taken from the latter source. Second in importance to these would be those volumes of the *Public Records of the Colony of Connecticut* and the *Public Records of the State of Connecticut* for the years 1773–1787 (Hartford, 1887–1945). My own *Roger Sherman's Connecticut* (Middletown, 1971) provides the most thorough description in print of Connecticut during the Confederation, and of its role in Congress. Peter Force's *American Archives* (Washington, 1837–53) contains much that is useful to the historian willing to search for it. Oscar Zeichner's *Connecticut's Years of Controversy* (Chapel Hill, 1949) is still the best account of the coming of the Revolution to Connecticut.

I have found useful a number of general treatments of the period. Among them are: E. James Ferguson, *The Power of the Purse* (Chapel Hill, 1961); Don Higginbottom, *The War of American Independence* (New York, 1971); Merril Jensen, *The Founding of A Nation* (New York, 1968); *The New Nation* (New York, 1958); and *The Articles of Confederation* (Madison, Wisc., 1940); Edmund S. and Helen M. Morgan, *The Stamp Act Crisis,* (Chapel Hill, 1953); Robert Taylor, "Trial at Trenton," *The William and Mary Quarterly*, 3rd Series, XXVI (October, 1969), 521–547; and Christopher Ward, *The War of the Revolution* (New York, 1952).

I have depended to a very great extent on a number of unpublished doctoral dissertations and masters' theses. In alphabetical order they are: Bonnie Bromberger Collier, "Connecticut's Standing Order and its Political Opposition, 1783–1800" (University of Connecticut, 1971); Larry R. Gerlach, "The Connecticut Delegates and the Continental Congress: From Confederation to Constitution, 1774–1789" (University of Nebraska, 1965); Herbert James Henderson, "Political Factions in the Continental Congress: 1774–1783" (Columbia University, 1962); Harvey Milton Wachtell, "The Conflict Between Localism and Nationalism in Connecticut, 1783–1788" (University of Missouri, 1971); William Floyd Willingham, "Windham, Connecticut: Profile of a Revolutionary Community, 1755–1818" (Northwestern University, 1972).

Of great help in writing profiles of delegates were the *Dictionary of American Biography* (New York, 1928–44); Franklin Bowditch Dexter, *Biographical Sketches of the Graduates of Yale College* (New York, 1885–1912); and Clifford Shipton, *Sibley's Harvard Graduates* (Cambridge, 1873–   ).

From time to time, though not frequently, I have quoted directly from manuscript sources. At the Connecticut Historical Society I used the Jeremiah Wadsworth, William Samuel Johnson, Oliver Wolcott, Sr., William Williams, and Jonathan Trumbull, Sr., Papers. The Wolcott Gibbs Lane Collection at Yale was useful in developing my sketch of Samuel Huntington.

To Larry Gerlach, Glenn Weaver, Judith Shiff, Robert Schnare, Frances Hoxie, Bonnie Collier, and the Reference Staff at Sterling Memorial Library at Yale, I express great thanks for help rendered and nary a growl.